20AMERICAN
PEAKS & CRAGS

20 AMERICAN PEAKS & CRAGS

THOMAS MORRISEY

cbi Contemporary Books, Inc.
Chicago

Library of Congress Cataloging in Publication Data

Morrisey, Thomas, 1952-
 Twenty American peaks and crags.

 Includes bibliographies and index.
  1. Mountaineering—United States.   2. Mountains—
United States.   I. Title.
GV199.4.M67   1978   796.5'22'0973   78-57464
ISBN 0-8092-7569-4
ISBN 0-8092-7568-6 pbk.

To Patricia

Copyright © 1978 by Trend Books, Inc.
All rights reserved
Published by Contemporary Books, Inc.
180 North Michigan Avenue, Chicago, Illinois 60601
Manufactured in the United States of America
Library of Congress Catalog Card Number: 78-57464
International Standard Book Number: 0-8092-7569-4 (cloth)
                                      0-8092-7568-6 (paper)

Published simultaneously in Canada by
Beaverbooks
953 Dillingham Road
Pickering, Ontario L1W 1Z7
Canada

Contents

Preface

As a climber, I have found that one's first visit to a climbing area can be a somewhat bewildering experience. Even the guidebooks often only add to the bewilderment, for although they may provide detailed route information, they often do not convey a feel for the area. This feel for the area, or sense of at-homeness, is successfully conveyed to a climber only after he has climbed at a place one or more times. Knowing certain things, however—such as how a crag or mountain was formed, who climbed it first and how they did it, and just where things are—can help a climber toward that sense of at-homeness. There are those, I realize, who take the opposite view, saying that the pioneering spirit of mountaineering is kept alive only by approaching a mountain with no foreknowledge, just as its first ascenders supposedly did, but I feel that such an attitude wastes climbing time, and can waste lives. True, the adventure is kept in a climb by having to look for one's route, and by having to find one's own hidden handholds, but at the other extreme, one cannot climb the Grand Teton until one knows where it is.

In this book, then, I have attempted to convey some basic information as well as history, anecdotes, and comments about 20 American peaks and crags. It is my hope that such material will help climbers visiting these popular spots to know each of them better and to feel more comfortable in it.

But this book has another purpose as well, and that is to present a panorama of American climbing. This country has areas exemplifying virtually every form of climbing, from small technical routes on low cliffs to major high-altitude expeditioneering on giant peaks in remote places. It has been my purpose, therefore, to include examples of the major identifiable aspects of climbing in this book, and to try to show how each unit relates to the whole, helping to form the unique and vibrant composite that is American climbing.

In this regard, I realize that in confining myself to 20 examples, I have overlooked equally important areas, and some may feel that my omission of places of major importance leaves gaps in this book. That may be so; perhaps a treatment of 2,000 American peaks and crags would have served my purpose better. However, it would have been a bit difficult to stuff such a book into a rucksack. In any case, I have made my choices, and I feel that I can live with them.

A special note should be made about our roles as climbers. Of the 20 areas discussed in this book, one has been closed to climbers and one may be demolished as the book goes to press. Action is necessary in order to retain or regain these areas as places in which we climbers can pursue our sport and in order to prevent other areas from being closed or destroyed. It is our duty as climbers to establish a spotless reputation for common sense and courtesy—qualities once universally associated with climbers, but vanishing as our numbers grow—so that we may be allowed to climb. It is also our duty to speak out to our legislators and our fellow citizens so that our nation's mountains and crags, places of rare beauty as well as climbing areas, will be preserved for posterity. Most climbers are climbers in part because they enjoy solitude. If we are to maintain solitude in the face of a climbing boom, we must keep as many cliffs and mountains as possible open and available to our use. It is my hope that by drawing attention to a closed area and an area that may soon be a gravel pit, I will be writing chapters in the histories of these places and not their epitaphs.

I should also note that although these chapters often discuss the history of a particular peak or crag, or comment extensively about one or two routes, this is not a guidebook to or a history of these places. For the former the reader should consult the individual guides to the areas treated, and for the latter there are numerous regional histories, as well as Chris Jones's very well-written *Climbing in North America*. For readers unfamiliar with climbing terms or rating systems, an explanation of the rating systems and a glossary of climbing terms are provided in the appendices to this book.

Finally, to give credit where credit is due, this book contains information gleaned from various sources, including interviews, letters, articles from *Off Belay*, *Climbing*, *Summit*, *North American Climber*, *Mountain*, *Backpacker*, and other periodicals, as well as books, pamphlets, and brochures. I often consulted Jones's book, as well as Clark's *Men, Myths, and Mountains*, Noyce and McMorrin's *World of Mountaineering*, Bueler's *Mountains of the World*, and Godfrey and Chelton's *Climb!*—the exact portions consulted are given in the chapter reference lists. As to the reference lists themselves, they combine the style of bibliographical entries with footnotelike page notations so that readers can use the lists to further their knowledge of each of the areas discussed. The reference lists also note letters I have received from notable American climbers, as well as telephone conversations and interviews I have had with such climbers. This is done because I either quoted from these letters or conversations or because I used information obtained from them which I could not find in any other source. In making use of printed matter, however, for purposes of accuracy I tried to cite only information that I had located in at least two sources.

Often not credited is the help I received from the U.S. National Park Service and the U.S. Forest Service. Suffice it to say that most of the places discussed here are situated in national parks, monuments, or forests, and that if it were not for the cooperation, information, and photographs provided by the National Park Service and the Forest Service, as well as by individual parks, monuments, and forests, this would be a very short book, indeed. The reader may assume that if the place discussed in a chapter is in a national preserve, the agency responsible for that preserve contributed substantially to the chapter.

But enough. Here is the book. I hope that the reader will find it useful as an introduction to the places it covers—places representative of some features of the nation which offers the climber more than any other nation on earth.

Acknowledgments

Writing a book is rarely a solitary enterprise, and this one was certainly not one of the exceptions. Working on it proved to me many times over the truth of that old saw about friends in need being friends indeed. I would particularly like to thank the following persons and organizations for the help they gave me in putting this book together.

Nona Albregt, Harvey A. Arnold, Pat Bessner, C. H. Burnett, Herb and Jan Conn, Bill Forrest, Bob Godfrey, Bruce Groves, Bill Hartough, George Hurley, Sue Huth, Huntley Ingalls, Jeff Lowe, Greg Lutz, Don Owens, Steve Ranck, Ed Rhudy, Rick Tapia, Julie Thal, Harriet Transue, Dick Williams, and Chuck Winger.

The Alaska State Historical Society, the Alaska State Division of Tourism, the Bob Culp Climbing School, Custer State Park (South Dakota), Fantasy Ridge Alpinism, Forrest Mountaineering, The Gendarme, H. H. Heindel Photography, the Mount Washington Valley Chamber of Commerce, the State of New Hampshire Division of Economic Development, the State of New Mexico Division of

Tourism, *Off Belay* magazine, Rock and Snow, the University of Toledo Department of Recreation and Leisure Education, and the University of Toledo Mountaineering Club.

And finally, a special thank-you to the people, parks, monuments, regional offices, and photo library of the U.S. National Park Service, and to the U.S. Forest Service, two agencies which went beyond the call of duty to help me whenever I was in need of photos or information.

Introduction
American Climbing

Although the instinct is often criticized or civilized out of him, deep inside, man is a climber. Anthropologists speculate that *Homo sapiens* is the latest step in an evolutionary descent from the tree-dwelling primates. Perhaps this is why men seek heights. Perhaps there are other, more complex reasons.

As soon as a child learns to crawl, it starts to climb. Its desire to reach high places is as strong as, or stronger than, its desire to walk. Proceeding from the personal man to the social man, we find even more evidence concerning the height fixation of humans. In virtually every society, high places are credited with supernatural powers.

In the Far East, mountains have traditionally been places of retreat and meditation, where the individual can retire to seek spiritual enlightenment. In the golden age of Greece, the gods were believed to dwell on Mount Olympus. Aboriginal peoples of all continents have attached great significance to great rocks and peaks. A Havasupai legend links the tribe's destiny to two stone pinnacles on the walls of the Grand Canyon. When the pinnacles fall, the tribe will perish.

In Wyoming, the Sioux tribe gathered annually at a great stone intrusion to worship the sun-god from it in a ceremony of dance and song. Today that intrusion is called Sundance Mountain. In Australia, a gigantic stone in the desert is viewed in aboriginal legend as a source of life and knowledge. Africa's Kilimanjaro is endowed with similar powers by native legend. There is also good reason to believe that many of the highest peaks in the Front Range of America's Rocky Mountains were first ascended by the Ute and other Indians, although no one knows exactly why the Indians climbed these peaks.

The crags of England were often focal points of Druid culture, while in continental Europe the legends and folklore concerning the heights are as numerous as the Alps. Every alpinist knows, for example, about the Eiger; but few know that the mountain's name means "ogre." Early travelers in the Alps returned with stories of great dragons and evil beings. When Christianity came into being, high mountains became sites for monasteries, and it was not uncommon for travelers to place small shrines on high peaks and passes.

As man became more civilized, and thus more occupied with war, military objectives became a good excuse for climbing mountains. Great ranges were crossed to enable armies to spring sneak attacks, high summits were pressed into service as observation posts, and clifftops were used for their impregnability as fortress sites. If doing all of these things involved some measure of aesthetics as well, this was icing on the cake and no cause for complaint.

In the 19th century, as industry and science leaped forward on all fronts, British and continental European climbers appeared in ever-increasing numbers, and the golden age of Alpinism saw practically all the continental peaks conquered. The reasons given for engaging in this mountain-climbing activity were patriotism and scientific interest. Men supposedly went through hardships and risked their lives in order to take barometric readings, chart topographies, study fauna, and hang a national banner from an ice ax in the snowy isolation of a geographic high point. It was an age of sensibility, and very few would admit to climbing because they liked to. Yet, even after the first ascents, men came to climb the European peaks. For whatever reason, the urge to climb had been freshly awakened in Western man.

In the 19th century, Americans were still discovering their land. The areas of the East, already long settled, had incorporated the Eastern hills and mountains into various cultures. In isolated and quaint communities, superstitions had already been spun concerning the local cliffs and crags. Near the large metropolitan areas, a tradition of going to hill-country resorts, "to take the mountain air," had already been established. A hardy few were even already climbing the more hazardous ways up the higher mountains and cliffs.

In 1820, with the discovery and ascent of Pikes Peak, and the reports from government surveys that great mountains existed in the western interior, a great and renewed interest in mountains swept across this country. Climbers were recognized as national heroes, decorated by the government, and valued as role models for small boys. An aura of mystery and romance was woven around the high peaks. It was reported that they were higher than the Alps, and it was rumored that they were the highest mountains in the world. In the interests of surveying the mountainlands for a route to the Pacific, and of investigating the rumors of gold beneath the snowy summits, many of the Rockies in Colorado, Wyoming, and the surrounding area were climbed within the next few decades. Less was known about the great peaks far to the north. In 1867, with the purchase of Alaska from Russia, Americans had reason for a more intense interest in what had become their highest mountains. For various reasons, those would have to be climbed too.

The pioneer American climbers came in various degrees of skill and daring. A few American mountaineers had learned to climb in Europe, but for the most part the pioneer climbers were soldiers, surveyors, and trappers whose interest outstripped their experience, forcing them to climb by (and often on) the seat of their pants. During the 19th century, more trained climbers and guides began to appear, but many of these concentrated their efforts in the Canadian Rockies, then nicknamed the "Canadian Alps." Clubs began to form in the United States, however, for the expressed purpose of climbing mountains. Although many of these organizations concentrated on peaks with an elevation of 14,000 feet or more, the message was still apparent. Climbing as a pastime was beginning to take hold in America.

In the early years of this century, climbing was dominated by Europeans. The majority of Americans who climbed were still mystified by roped belays. Altitude seemed to be the primary concern, and the easiest way up was generally thought of as the best. Relatively few people appreciated a hard climb for the climb's sake, and those who did often climbed in questionable safety, knowing little or nothing of protection techniques.

As the 20th century progressed, so did the climbers. On the East Coast several mountaineering tigers gained experience in international climbing, and began to push harder new routes up both climbed and unclimbed peaks in the United States. In California, new rope techniques developed by the Rock Climbing Section of the Sierra Club enabled climbers to take falls in safety, opening ever harder routes to consideration. And when World War II necessitated the training of mountain troops during the '40s, new equipment, technique, and camaraderie left American climbers even better prepared for peacetime climbing. As the '50s opened, American climbing had ascended to a level equal with that of climbing anywhere in the world.

Yet, it was not just the climbers who made American climbing what it is today. It was also the quality, the variety, and the sheer quantity of the crags and summits of this country.

This is really the decisive factor in the modern excellence of U. S. climbing—American climbers have any type of climb they want within their own national boundaries. Climbers with a penchant for small but difficult crags have their choice of hundreds of small cliffs throughout the country. In the realm of more classic mountain climbing, the Appalachians, the Western Rockies, and the West Coast volcanoes have something for every taste. Hard and prolonged rock climbing has become an American specialty, with long climbs on isolated monoliths and even longer climbs on the great and steep faces so well described by the simple term *big wall*. And, for those who desire the ultimate in altitude and raw elemental force, the giant peaks of Alaska compare favorably with any high mountains in the world, and are considered to be in a class with the Himalayan ranges.

The American climber today is a highly refined creature, the product of several types of evolution. From his fellow American climbers, he has gained the technology to climb better than ever before. From the European climbing tradition, he has gained the custom of climbing for sport. And from some time-lost primal man, he has acquired a sense of awe for the mountains, evidenced in the grand rush of emotion that seems unavoidable when he first views a great peak or a fine crag. Here, perhaps, is one of the ultimate triumphs: to stand on top of that which has such power. So inspired, this country's climbers continue to pioneer in the frontiers of eagles and clouds. Who can say what the morrow may bring?

Part 1
Crags, Outcrops, and Canyons

In the European tradition of mountaineering, the smaller rock areas close to a climber's home were looked upon as a practice area—as a kind of bull pen used by the climber before he stepped onto the playing field of the Alps. Neither rock climbing nor the style with which one climbed were considered of great importance. What mattered was to mount a summit, and if a high summit could be gained by walking, so much the better. The climbers of earlier days often passed hard sections by having a strong guide haul away on a stout rope above. The few men who dared to seek difficult paths in the mountains were viewed as dangerous fools by their contemporaries.

As the times changed, as first ascents became harder to come by, and as greater hazards had to be faced by those who wished to pioneer, changes also occurred in the nature of rock climbing. Harder rock climbs were sought in order to temper climbers for the greater challenges they would face in the Alps. But the local crag was still considered a training ground, not as a challenge in and of itself.

When climbing came to America, the New World's

impressive abundance of high peaks prompted a spectrum of climber attitudes. Many climbers were content to walk up the "Fourteeners" of Colorado and thus gain glory without taking chances; some climbers sought harder summits; and European climbers, used to a stiffer grade and hungry for first ascents, clamored for the opportunity to test themselves against difficult and unclimbed mountains.

Like the European crags, the American crags served both as places to stretch one's legs and socialize before going off to the mountains and as gymnasiums of sorts in which climbers could hone their skills. But in America, crags also came to perform a third function.

The United States had mountains in abundance, but these were all lumped together far from the centers of population. For those who wished to climb but could not travel to the peaks, an alternative was sought in smaller cliffs and crags close to home. As a result, these cliffs and crags were regarded with a new seriousness.

Today the smaller rock formations of this country are producing climbers of unparalleled ability, many of whom will never stand on a mountain peak. Some wish to climb only boulders. But others, in revival of an old climbing tradition, are taking skills learned on the friendly rock of home and applying those skills to rocks, cliffs, and mountains of ever-increasing height. The crag climbing of today thus serves a two-fold purpose. Challenging routes test the upper limits of a climber's abilities while preparing him for unseen tests on higher horizons. Here, then, are the forerunners in the search for climbing's new extremes— mounting the crags and "practice rocks" which catch the first light of climbing's new dawn.

1

The Trapps
of the Shawangunks

To the Western climber, much of climbing has to do with mountains. Those who venture onto rock in Colorado, Wyoming, and the West Coast do so in the knowledge that snowy summits are only hours, and sometimes minutes, away. Until quite recently this situation led to a polarized view of Western climbing in general; following routes to the top of a mountain was considered "real" climbing, while clambering about on the smaller cliffs was thought of as "practice" climbing—secondary, and in some way inferior.

Eastern climbers were spared such notions. The mountains of the Eastern states are rather like the teeth of an old horse, worn smooth and low. Almost all are readily accessible to any determined hiker. One stands on their summits in the company of tourists with cheap cameras, and technical routes to these summits are almost unknown.

With only worn and low mountains at his disposal, the East Coast climber has traditionally turned to cliffs rather than peaks. The Northeast, especially, has become the land of rock climbers, so much so that many climbers from this region have never climbed more than a Grade III route, and have no inclination to do so. This is an area which has been able to appreciate a technically difficult rock route for years.

In such an atmosphere, a challenging section of cliff, no matter how small, quickly develops a following after a few pioneer ascents have been made. A cliff of any size will draw climbers from several states, and a major area with technically severe routes will become a nerve center and a trend setter. Such an area is the Shawangunks, near the village of New Paltz, New York.

Credit for discovering the climbing potential of the Shawangunks goes to Fritz Weissner, who sighted the cliffs from a distance while climbing near the Hudson River with members of the Appalachian Mountain Club (AMC). Weissner, who was later to open both the Needles of South Dakota and Devils Tower in Wyoming to modern rock climbing, opened the Shawangunks as well. Like most climbing areas in America, the Shawangunks saw little activity during World War II and a boom in activity once the war ended. Weissner's discovery of the cliffs, and the founding of a Rock Climbing Section of the AMC by Herb and Jan Conn, made the area almost the property of the Appalachian Mountain Club. There was climbing activity in several sections of cliffs, including Millbrook Mountain, the Bayards, and Skytop, but the cliff destined to become the most popular with climbers was the Trapps (from the Dutch word *treppen*, or "steps"). The Trapps is the longest continuous cliff section in the "Gunks," lies literally a stone's throw from Route 44–55 (a major highway), and has a wide and level carriage road at its base, making the cliff ultra-accessible to climbers. The AMC, led by Weissner and his partner, Hans Kraus, took advantage of this accessibility to open several difficult routes on Trapps, an example being Weissner and Kraus's *High Exposure*, done in 1941 and now rated 5.6.

After World War II, as word of AMC activity in the

area got around, other groups began to trickle into the Shawangunks. Outing and mountaineering clubs from Princeton, Harvard, and other universities visited the area and became regulars. It came as a surprise to the AMC and the Ivy Leaguers when Art Gran and a small following from the City College of New York moved in and began to raise the standards of climbing on the cliffs. Aid routes were freed, and more and more climbs were established at the 5.8 rating. The cliff near Trapps (called "Near Trapps") saw the next stage of progression, as *Never Never Land* in 1959 opened 5.9 climbing in the Gunks. This was answered on the Trapps by the freeing of *Retribution* at 5.10 in 1961. The climber in both cases was Jim McCarthy, a Princetonian who climbed at or above the level set by the CCNY group, yet hailed from the Ivy League's side of the tracks.

Gran and company were generous with their contempt for the "Appies." In a way, the two groups symbolized the continuation of two Old World climbing traditions. Like the continental European climbers, the AMC and its associates were somewhat refined and took their climbing as a mixed tonic of intellectual insight and physical activity. The CCNY group resembled the climbers of Scotland and Wales, with a taste for wild night-before-the-climb parties and general sarcasm. To erase any doubt as to which side of the fence they stood on, these Gunks climbers named themselves the "Vulgarians."

Appearing as they did in the late '50s and early '60s, the Vulgarians found it easy to identify with the radicalism then sweeping the country. Bob Dylan's music formed the background sound for many of their climbs, and the Vulgarians' total effect was something like that of a rock 'n' roll band on a cliff face. The Vulgarians developed followings of young girls, some of the first "climbing groupies" in the country, and adopted extremism as a way of life. On the cliffs, they pushed the climbing levels closer to the fine edge, and back in camp their revelry followed the same lines in pursuit of almost every sort of excess. At times the Vulgarians combined extremism in climbing with other excesses. A favorite Vulgarian stunt was to speed-climb the classic roadside climbs in the nude. By the time police responded to the complaints of passing motorists, a climb had been completed and the vertical streakers were noisily celebrating the feat at a nearby campground. AMC attempts to work with the owners of the cliffs to regulate climbing only resulted in more friction and greater Vulgarian atrocities.

In 1963 the bulk of the Shawangunks came under the authority of the Mohonk Trust, a private, nonprofit organization formed to ensure the use of the area for recreation requiring no alteration of the land. Rock climbing fell into this category, and the use of the cliffs for climbing was continued, as was a land-use fee initiated after a climbing fatality in 1958. Things began to settle down just a little bit, and in 1964 Art Gran wrote the first guidebook for the area.

The guidebook announced the start of a new era, as such publications almost always do. A former gymnast named Dick Williams appeared at the cliffs, freeing the old aid routes and putting up hard new free ascents with acro-

Russ Raffa on *Shockley's Ceiling* (5.5) at the Trapps, in New York's Shawangunks. (Photo by Harvey A. Arnold)

batic swings not seen before in East Coast climbing. In 1967 another strong young climber made a name for himself, as John Stannard freed *Foops* on Skytop, which turned out to be one of the most spectacular 5.10s in the country. As the '70s drew near, the Gunks began to sport contingents of dedicated women who continued the female Shawangunks climbing tradition started by Bonnie Prudeen in the early '50s. At the forefront of this group were Gerd Thuestad, Eve Uiga, and Evy Goldstone.

Contemporary climbing in the Shawangunks continues to be of an extraordinarily high caliber. The Trapps was again the center of attention in recent years, when Barbara Bein became one of the first women to lead 5.10 in the Gunks, including *Retribution*, a Trapps classic, and *Cheap Thrills* and *Keep on Struttin'*. Others have continued the parade of 5.9 and 5.10 climbs on the cliff. *Kansas City*, once a classic Williams aid climb on Near Trapps, is now free at 5.12, and on the Mohonk side of Skytop a Steve Wunsch creation called *Supercrack* has only been repeated once as of this writing. Estimates of its difficulty go anywhere from 5.11 to 5.14(!), although all concerned agree that it is very, very hard.

The popularity of the Trapps turns it into a carnival on weekends and holidays, when hundreds of climbers swarm over the more-than-mile-long cliff. On such days, with food vendors strolling along the highway, cars double-parked in the small spaces available, and climbers falling off just about every route as far as one can see, it is usually best to climb somewhere else. It does not, however, always have to be that way.

I remember a very hot Tuesday in the middle of a recent August when I counted six other climbers on the whole of Trapps. I was with a nonclimbing companion and had gone in the hope of finding someone to climb with. Instead, I had to give a quick lesson on belaying, and proceed to do the routes by placing protection, climbing, placing more protection, downclimbing, removing protection . . .

The thing to remember is that the Trapps is filled with climbers and watchers on weekends and national holidays, particularly in fair weather. For those interested in seeing where and how the difficult climbs are done, such an atmosphere may be what's needed. Those desiring solitude should wait for midweek or bad weather.

Either way, the Shawangunks are easier to find than most climbing areas. They are in downstate New York, close to Pennsylvania, New Jersey, Connecticut, and Massachusetts. As one drives north on the New York State Thruway from New York City and approaches exit 18, the cliffs will appear in the early morning sun as great golden-white bands lining the western horizon. Going into New Paltz, the visitor would be wise to stop at Rock and Snow, the local emporium de climb, to pick up a copy of the guidebook *Shawangunk Rock Climbs*, by Dick Williams. Route 299 is then taken west out of town to Route 44–55, where, after pleasant moments of driving off the road while staring at the overhangs, the climber will come to a U-turn below the Trapps. Climbers usually park here or at one of the pullouts down the road (on crowded days it is usually best to have someone drop you at the cliffs). To get to the cliff proper, the climber walks uphill along the highway from the U-turn to a place where a pipe drains a spring at the roadside below the cliff.

This is the beginning of a very short path to the Uberfall, a sort of Trapps social center, complete with first-aid station, bulletin board, running spring, and a pool that is often pressed into use as a beverage cooler on hot days. Questions can be asked here, or delivered to the Mohonk Trust ranger, who may be attired in anything from a ragged Chouinard Equipment T-shirt to a uniform, but will be friendly and polite either way, and will also sell the climber a climbing permit. The permit fee helps preserve the Gunks for climbers and others, and although there are those who will avoid the ranger so as not to pay the fee, doing this can only jeopardize the future of climbing on the Gunks.

Navigation around the Trapps is relatively simple. As the climber walks up to the Uberfall, he comes out onto a wide and firm path called the Undercliff Road, which was a carriage road in days gone by. With the guidebook in hand, it is easy to pick out climbs once one or two of the principal landmarks have been identified by the ranger or a local climber. Near the Uberfall, many of the climbs start from the road, but farther down a short section of talus must be crossed to reach the starts of climbs. Cairns on top of the cliff mark many of the descent routes, and the guidebook lists the others.

As to the climbing itself, only two things need be mentioned, namely, gritstone and overhangs.

Shawangunks gritstone is the name for the quartz conglomerate rock of which the cliffs consist. This rock, formed in layered horizontal deposits, is relatively hard, and it seems especially secure to climbers who have been reared on a diet of shale and sandstone. The layered nature of the rock resulted in horizontal weaknesses, which broke some deposits away to form the legendary Shawangunks overhangs, and it seems as though every climb, even the easiest, has at least one of these overhangs. Climbers on some routes will encounter several overhangs in sequence, like an inverted stairwell. This can be a chilling obstacle to those not used to it, and in addition to style many of the climbs in the Gunks require a fair degree of arm strength.

With more than 250 recorded climbs on the Trapps alone, it is difficult to pick out any one climb as recommended, but beginning climbers generally will enjoy *Boston* (5.3), near the Uberfall, and *Belly Roll* (5.3), farther down, while more advanced climbers will find a host of Trapps classics, including the *Horseman* (5.4), *Frog's Head* (5.5), *Miss Bailey* (5.6), *Gorilla My Dreams* (5.7), *Shockley's Ceiling* (5.5), and the *Overhanging Layback* (5.7).

Some of the better-known Trapps 5.8s are the short *Dirty Gerdie*, *Son of Easy O*, and *Absurdland*, one of Jim McCarthy's many "land" climbs. Those who wish to test the upper extremes of climbing on the Trapps should take a look at *Doug's Roof* (5.11) or try the static variation of

Worp Factor 1 (5.10) or any of the dozens of problems on the boulders along the carriage road.

Style and ethics are major concerns in the Gunks. The established routes can be climbed with chocks only—if a bolt or a pin is needed, it should already be there, and it is considered good form to use only chocks on new routes as well.

The popularity and high standards of climbing in the Shawangunks is reflected in the fact that most of the great North American climbers have climbed there and that new frontiers continually fall there, a claim that only the Gunks and Yosemite can make with regularity. The Shawangunks have seen some of the hardest climbing in the world. These gritstone cliffs stand as a monument to what climbers without mountains can do.

References

Dumais, Richard. "Shawangunks: The North-East's Most Popular Crag." *Mountain*, no. 21 (May 1972), pp. 23–27.

Jones, Chris. *Climbing in North America*. Berkeley: University of California Press for American Alpine Club, 1976. Pp. 213–218, 371–73.

Rubin, Al. "Shawangunks." *Mountain*, no. 32 (February 1974), p. 11.

Rubin, Al. "Shawangunks." *Mountain*, no. 53 (January/February 1977), pp. 14–15.

Williams, Richard C. *Shawangunk Rock Climbs*. New York: American Alpine Club, 1972.

Williams, Dick. "Shawangunks." *North American Climber*, July 1975, pp. 8–9.

Williams, Dick. "Shawangunks." *North American Climber*, November 1975, p. 9.

Williams, Dick. "Shawangunks." *North American Climber*, Winter 1977, p. 8.

2

Cathedral Ledge

Granite is by no means only a commodity of the Western states. New Hampshire is nicknamed the "Granite State" with very good reason, some prime pieces of evidence being the cliffs of the Mount Washington Valley near the town of North Conway. These cliffs include Eagle Ledge, Woodchuck Ledge, Humphrey's Ledge, White's Ledge, and the flowing friction slabs of White Horse Ledge. From a technical rock climber's point of view, however, the first among the cliffs is Cathedral Ledge, immediately west of North Conway.

The reasons for the exceptional climbing on Cathedral go back more than 150 million years, to its creation as an igneous intrusion far underground. The intrusion cooled slowly, with only a few faults or joints, and some of these were refilled by later igneous material. Erosion then removed the matter on top of the intrusions, relieving pressure and allowing the rock to expand and crack in roughly horizontal sheets, in a process known to geologists as exfoliation. The next major action that occurred was glacial movement against the ends of these exfoliated

Like many popular Eastern crags, Cathedral Ledge is easy to reach by highway and is in a popular recreational area. (Photo by Dick Smith, courtesy state of New Hampshire)

sheets, movement which ground material away and thus created the cliff face. Because of varying degrees of hardness in the rock, this glacial movement produced ledges and overhangs in some places, whereas in other places the rock was polished quite smoothly.

The result is a cliff face with a pleasant mixture of climbing features, arranged in such a manner that the average rating of Cathedral Ledge climbs is quite respectable. Yet Cathedral was passed over by climbers for quite some time. Trails were built to either side of the Ledge, and a road was put in up the back side, complete with tourist observation deck at the top, but it was not until the late 1950s that serious climbing began on this great granite crescent. For an East Coast cliff, this was a rather late start.

Climbing has long been associated with students and academics, and Cathedral is quite accessible to the Eastern university belt. The tone of the area, quiet and scenic, is one that appeals to climbers, and the rock is hard and solid, always a desirable feature. One can only assume that the climbers of the region could not, to reverse the saying, see the tree for the forests. Granite buffs were lured to the larger cliff on Cannon Mountain; climbers with a penchant for ice could find it in the Mount Washington ravines; and

A climber starts a route on Cathedral Ledge. (Photo by Dave Ingemie, courtesy Mount Washington Valley Chamber of Commerce)

the focus for Eastern rock climbing tended to be (and still tends to be) on the Shawangunks.

Whatever the reason for the late start, when serious rock climbing began at Cathedral Ledge, it began with a bang. In 1959, the British-Canadian free-climbing specialist John Turner and the Shawangunks veteran Art Gran teamed up to pioneer a route called *Repentance*, at 5.9, if you please! At that time, putting up a climb of that grade was remarkable anywhere in the country. Doing so outside of California was unheard of. *Repentance* far exceeded two earlier skirmishes onto the Ledge—the *Standard Route* (5.6) of 1931, and D'Arcy and Coffin's *Thin Air* (5.5) of 1955. Moreover, Turner proved that the 5.9 was more than a mere fluke when he returned the next year with Richard Wilmott to climb *Recompense*, at the same rating.

Thus began a Cathedral Ledge reputation for hard climbs. In the early 60s, Turner, Wilmott, Joe Cote, John Reppy, and others began to trace a network of routes onto Cathedral Ledge. Free moves above the 5.7 level were common, and most routes involved the use of aid.

This surge of hard climbing on Cathedral Ledge continued for a little more than ten years, until the '70s ushered in a new movement centered on the elimination of aid moves and the use of nuts for protection. Spearheading this movement was a teenager from Boston named Henry Barber. In the fall of 1971, Barber free-climbed a former A1 route in the section on the right side of Cathedral called the Practice Aid Slab. When he had finished, Cathedral Ledge had its first 5.10.

The following year, Barber, Bob Anderson, and British-born Paul Ross swept like a bold new wave over the aid routes of Cathedral. Intimidating routes such as the *Grim Reaper* (5.10) showed the new style at its best, and in the autumn of 1972, Barber, now referred to by one and all as "Hot Henry," upped the ante even further with the establishment of *Lichen Delight*, a 5.11.

Perhaps the most novel achievement of 1972, however, was a Henry Barber and Paul Ross creation called *The Big Plum*. This was a climb done in a British tradition called a girdle traverse, which Ross had learned in the Lake District. The object was to start at one end of the cliff and cross the cliff, finishing at the upper corner of the opposite end. Ross did considerable climbing on Cathedral, always checking for traverse possibilities. Finally, thinking such a route possible after a successful girdle of White Horse Ledge, he suggested the climb to the ever-game Barber.

The climb took two days. The route was a 33-pitch Grade V, more than 3,000 feet in length. The hardest free moves were at the 5.10 level, and Barber reported that the route had no aid, although he added somewhat confusingly that seven rappels and three pendulum swings were involved. Yet, regardless of disputes over the fine points of what constitutes aid, *The Big Plum* was a fine route, and it helped to touch off an American girdling tradition. Running north to south, the *Plum* crossed and incorporated into its path sections of *Recluse* (5.10), *They Died Laughing* (5.8), *Diedre Direct* (5.9), *Remission* (5.7), *Abracadabra* (5.7), *Pendulum* (5.9), *Standard* (5.6), *Thin Air* (5.5), *Recompense* (5.9), *The Beast 666* (5.8), and *Nutcracker* (5.9). In addition, the route intersected with *Karen's Variation, The Last Temptation, Diedre, The British Are Coming, Angel's Highway, Repentance, Antline, Cathedral Direct, Mordor*

Cathedral Ledge overhangs, products of the exfoliation process, are famous for classic aid routes, many of which have recently gone free. (Photo courtesy Mount Washington Valley Chamber of Commerce)

Wall, and the *Great Chimney.* Those who delight in understatement could call *The Big Plum* a good two days' work.

In 1973, Barber, Anderson, and John Bragg made the first free ascent of *Airation,* a finger-killing 5.11, and Barber and Bragg also established the marginally less difficult *Chockline* (5.10).

In 1975, the inevitable happened when Ross, this time accompanied by a young Connecticut climber named Doug Madara, made the reverse traverse (south to north) of Cathedral Ledge, a Grade V 5.9 called *King Crab,* which broke 2,000 feet of new ground. Madara, only 18 years old, had not been climbing very long. In Mount Washington Valley tradition, he was nicknamed "Devastating Doug" for *King Crab* and other achievements.

Climbers who wish to find Cathedral Ledge can get to North Conway on State Route 16. They should remember that they are looking for *North* Conway, and not East Conway, Center Conway, or Conway. Parking is available just minutes from the ledge, and on Cathedral itself navigation is fairly simple once one can locate a few principal features, such as the various roofs and chimneys. Perimeter travel is equally simple, with trails to each side of the cliff and a road coming down from the top for those who want to do it in style and be met by the limo at the end of the climb.

As the area is somewhat tourist-oriented, there are several campgrounds and motels within easy driving distance of Cathedral Ledge. Those who have traveled cross-country to get to the Ledge, and then discover that they have left half of the equipment at home, will be gratified to know that International Mountain Equipment, a climbing shop on Main Street in North Conway, can provide them with both the equipment and the information that they may need.

Cathedral is especially popular for rock climbing, though in good winters ice climbing is done there as well. For information on the former it is wise to consult Joseph Cote's *A Climber's Guide to Mount Washington Valley* and Henry Barber's *1973 Supplement* to this guide. As for regulations, there are none, though clean climbing is firmly accepted by the local climbers, and should be by visitors as well. The authorities request only that climbers avoid littering and campfires.

References

Barber, Henry. *A Climber's Guide to Mount Washington Valley: 1973 Supplement*. Topsfield, Mass.: Fox Run Press, 1973.

Cote, Joseph. *A Climber's Guide to Mount Washington Valley.* Topsfield, Mass.: Fox Run Press, 1972.

Ross, Paul. "The Nature of New England Climbing." *Mountain,* no. 21 (May 1972), pp. 19–22.

Ross, Paul. "Cathedral Ledge." *North American Climber,* November 1975, p.7.

Ross, Paul. "Go Sideways, Young Man!" *Climbing,* May/June 1976, pp. 24–26.

Rubin, Al. "New England." *Mountain,* no. 32 (February 1974), p. 11.

Rubin, Al. "New Hampshire 1975, 1976." *Mountain,* no. 53, (January/February 1977), pp.16–17.

Webster, Ed. "Down East: A Survey of New Hampshire Free Climbing." *Climbing,* May/June 1976, pp. 8–22.

3

Seneca Rock

The Potomac Highlands, in the eastern portion of West Virginia, are a rugged area of river knobs and valleys, formed by the faulting and folding of an ancient ocean bed. The broken sandstone arches of this bed have weathered and been exposed as long and narrow cliffs and crags on steep and forested ridgetops. One of the largest of these crags is Seneca Rock, a striking formation rising almost 900 feet above the North Fork of the South Branch of the Potomac River. Because of the durable nature of its quartz-laden Tuscarora sandstone, Seneca has resisted the forces of wind and rain well, with 300 feet of rock face rising from the timber and scree at its base.

Approached from the north, on West Virginia Route 28, or from the south, on Route 33, Seneca appears at first to be an exposed cliff line on the side of a hill. It gradually detaches itself and stands out as the isolated formation it is as one nears the base of the rock. Coming from the east on Route 33, one rounds a curve to get a dramatic first view of Seneca Rock, standing loftily and defiant at the intersection of two valleys. The tiny village of Mouth of

Seneca Rock, as seen from the village Mouth of Seneca. (Photo by Bruce Groves)

Seneca, where Routes 28 and 33 meet, yields the best view of Seneca, one of the most photographed landmarks in the state of West Virginia.

Standing in the parking circle at the 28–33 intersection, the visitor sees Seneca as a sharp, almost Gothic, skyline. To the north, or left, is the rock's true summit, the North Peak. This peak is reachable by hiking trail or horse, and it is popular with backpackers and tourists for its view.

From the North Peak, the skyline runs south to a deep and broad depression known as the Gunsight Notch, in the middle of which stands a slender blade of rock called the Gendarme. The ridge ascends rapidly to the right of the Gendarme, past a small gargoyle (the Gryphon's Beak) to the South Peak, inaccessible to horse or hiker, and therefore considered the mountaineer's summit of Seneca Rock. The downsloping ridge running to the right from the South Peak is interrupted twice by projecting formations, the Cockscomb and Humphrey's Head, before the South End takes a steep plunge into Roy Gap. Across the gap, a tall but narrow cliff on a ridge end, appropriately called the Southern Pillar, is technically a separate formation, but it is so obviously a part of the same rock band as Seneca that climbers consider it to be a subformation.

Describing the first ascent of Seneca can be a bit confusing, since one must clarify which peak is being discussed and what qualifies as a first ascent. The first

The South End and the Southern Pillar, on a typically misty Potomac Highlands morning. (Photo by Greg Lutz)

The Southern Pillar. (Photo by Don Owens)

climbers of the North Peak and the Southern Pillar are lost to history, since these summits are so accessible that countless scouts and hunters must have stood upon them before mountaineers came to Seneca. Even the climbers' summit, the South Peak, offers a choice of first-ascenders.

The Seneca Indians attributed the feat to one Princess Snowbird, a coy and sprightly boulderer in buckskin who grew proficient at climbing and announced that she would marry none but the bravest of warriors—the man who could follow her to the top of the rock. She then made what would be considered a daring first ascent by even the most modern standards, an on-sight free solo in bare feet or, at most, moccasins. The braves who pursued her had their problems. Most were forced to retreat; a few of the hard men pressed on and fell to their deaths; and the one brave who neared the top began to slip only inches from his goal, this being far back in the days before EBs and chalk. At that point, Snowbird, no doubt envisioning a lingering spinsterhood, not to mention a cold bivouac, reached out and brought her husband-to-be to the summit ledge, one of the world's narrower and more exposed trysting places. However, despite the fanfare and the dramatic nature of her climb, mountaineers must deny the princess a first ascent on three counts:

1. She failed to build a cairn or otherwise leave evidence of her ascent.
2. She failed to give a record of the actual route taken to the summit.
3. She brought up her second on direct aid—a serious breach of ethics on this otherwise fine ascent!

Discounting poor Princess Snowbird, then, a long jump into the 20th century is necessary before any evidence of an ascent is found. In the late 1930s, climbers found this inscription in the rock of the summit: "DB Sept 16, 1906." The inscription is believed to have been made by D. Bittinger, a surveyor-cartographer who was doing work for the National Park Service in the area at that time. The summit inscription was thought to have been lost, but in 1974 it was rediscovered by a party led by Donald Hubbard, who reported the find in an April 1976 *Off Belay* article, complete with a photo of the faint and elusive record. Because of unmistakable evidence of the climb, Bittinger's ascent is believed to be the first, although the details of his route and his party were never recorded.

Another account of an early climb to the top of Seneca Rock comes from "Buck" Harper, owner of a local general store, who tells of a route his father found after several

A climber comes to grips with *Ye Gods and Little Fishes*, 5.8 on the South End. (Photo by Don Owens)

abortive attempts. The route Harper describes is the *Old Ladies' Route*, which, at a rating of 5.1, is the easiest of the climbs to the South Peak. Ascending the notch between the Cockscomb and Humphrey's Head, this climb follows a traversing ledge and a large flake to the Summit Ledge, from which a long third-class ramp and a short fourth-class scramble lead to the South Peak summit. This is still a popular beginners' route, and it is often third-classed by more experienced climbers to gain access to the upper rock and to descend without having to rappel. The two-way traffic thus generated can be a problem for the climbers as well as a source of amusement to loungers on the Summit Ledge above, and Luncheon Ledge below.

A bit of climbing activity occurred during early years of the 20th century at Seneca, although not all of it was undertaken for purely aesthetic reasons. A local moonshiner and general ne'er-do-well attempted to dynamite the Gendarme in the '20s, apparently as a protest against Prohibition, but his blast was in vain. The Gendarme still stands, with a 5.4 line on its east side and a 5.8 line on its west side, but climbers may wish to contemplate the numerous fracture lines caused by the explosion in the Gendarme's base before attempting this surprisingly exposed climb.

In 1939, armed with nothing more lethal than some rope and climbing hardware, Paul Bradt, Samuel Moore, and Donald Hubbard (yes, the same Donald Hubbard who would later reascend Seneca to find DB's inscription) made the first climb to the top of the South Peak by the use of technical mountaineering methods. In a long climb on a cold April day, with all the route-finding problems that are still a feature of Seneca climbing, the party made their way to the top by a route which started at roughly the South End and traversed the Seneca skyline to the South Peak. The route was named *Skyline Traverse*, although only a small portion of it is still referred to by that name. A remarkable thing about this ascent is that the line it took followed the crux pitches of at least six modern

Seneca climbs, with difficulty ratings, in order, of 5.4, 5.3, 5.1, 5.3, 5.4, and 5.4. Considering the inclement weather experienced on the climb and the equipment carried (hard-lay rope, soft pitons, and one carabiner for each man), this trio's effort was very daring.

Bradt, Moore, and Hubbard climbed at Seneca again in the fall of 1939, establishing at least three more routes. Under normal circumstances, the rock could have been expected to go on in the usual tradition of eastern crags, attracting the odd college outing club or the recently arrived European climber, and eventually building a small following of area climbers.

That was not to happen, however. Only four short years after the first technical ascent of the South Peak, Seneca was to host a swarm of climbers, with routes being climbed every day. Such an increase in climbing activity was most unusual. It took a world war to bring it about.

As the United States became involved in World War II, it became obvious that there was a possibility of alpine warfare in southern and central Europe. An accelerated effort to produce an expanded Army Mountain Corps began, including glacier training at Mount Rainier and alpine training in Colorado. Seneca Rock and other crags nearby were chosen as training grounds for rock climbing.

As the Army channeled recruits with climbing experience, and as experienced mountaineers signed up for the corps, the ranks of the mountain troops became filled with rock climbers of varied technique and background. The effect of bringing together so many climbers was soon felt as the climbers shared styles, rope techniques, and equipment pointers. Their Army duty was also the first contact most of the corps members had with modern equipment, including Quartermaster Corps-designed angle pitons, aluminum carabiners, and nylon rope. The last was extremely important, since it proved to be more than ten times as dependable as manila rope, therefore opening up more difficult grades of climbing without significantly increasing risk. It was on the walls of Seneca that Army men first put nylon rope to use, as they trained for action in central Italy. The Army put up a great number of new routes on Seneca, but only a few were recorded. Others were temporarily lost to posterity, only to be discovered in later years when younger cragsmen would, to their chagrin, find lines of Army pitons running up the latter pitches of supposedly "new" routes. The Army was indeed generous with its hardware, leaving several thousand pitons of various shapes and designs in Seneca, many of which have since been pulled as souvenirs or have broken off because of constant use. A good number still remain, however. The Face of a Thousand Pitons was so named because of its bristling appearance after the war, and it is curious to note that many modern Seneca climbers, the author included, have fallen and been spared by Army pins that were driven into Seneca before the climbers were born.

After the war ended and the mountain troops were discharged, many of them returned to their training area–playground on vacations and weekend trips, and during the postwar years a climbing community began to form at Seneca Rock. Regular pilgrimages to the rock were made by many mountaineering clubs; among them were some fine climbers from the Potomac Appalachian Trail Club, with its newly formed Rock Climbing Section. The Cleveland Mountaineers were also regulars, as were the Explorers of Pittsburgh, who put a register on the South Peak and drew up the first Seneca route list. As Seneca became known, climbers from the more established New England and East Coast areas began to visit it. Friendly rivalries developed, and routes of increased difficulty appeared.

The last few years have brought activity of extremely high standards to Seneca, with climbers such as John Stannard, Herb Laeger, and Eve Uiga leading the way to the upper levels of rock climbing. Several climbs of 5.10 difficulty have been recorded at the Gendarme, the local climbing shop, and although the area has no 5.11s as of

The South End, overhanging and exposed, is drawing increased attention as Seneca standards grow higher. (Photo by Don Owens)

this writing, one route, *Terra Firma Homesick Blues*, is a very high 5.10, and another, *Malevolence*, may be upgraded to 5.11 after a number of parties have climbed it and compared notes. There is little doubt that in the future more high-standard routes will be established at Seneca.

The climber visiting Seneca today would be wise to avoid the rock on holiday weekends, when many of the routes have waiting lines at the bottom. The rock is quite crowded during the summer, though the best climbing weather is usually in the fall. The town of Mouth of Seneca is well suited for a climbing visit. Although small, it has a climbing shop, general stores and gas stations, three restaurants, two motels, and two private campgrounds. Forest Service campgrounds are nearby; a state-owned park provides some parking and a picnic area; and despite the protests of climbers, a shiny new Visitors' Center, complete with asphalt parking area and a viewing station, was built recently. Also new is a suspension bridge for access to the rock over the North Fork. This replaced the old bridge, which gave up the ghost in 1976. A Seneca Rock campground and auditorium are being planned, although the plans may be shelved for environmental reasons.

Access to the rock is by Roy Gap Road, a dirt road that leads up to the swing bridge, after which another dirt road takes one up the gap. From this area, steep switch-backing trails lead to the bases of the various faces. A route guide is helpful, and *Seneca Rocks, W. Va.: A Climber's Guide*, by Rich Pleiss and Bill Webster is available. Also available is a guide pamphlet, printed on durable paper and showing only route lines and grades on photographs. The pamphlet is meant to put some adventure back into rock climbing through route-finding problems, and all profits from its sale go to help Seneca.

If further information is needed at the rock, climbers usually congregate around Luncheon Ledge, below Humphrey's Head, and the Summit Ledge, at the top of the *Old Ladies' Route*. The latest route information can be had by checking the new routes book at the Gendarme climbing shop.

A variety of degrees of difficulty can be found among the Seneca climbs. Novices will enjoy the *Old Ladies' Route* and its West Face counterpart, the *Old Man's Route*. Both are lengthy but easy, and both offer access to the summit. For those learning to lead, *Skyline Traverse* on the Southeast Corner and any of the climbs on Humphrey's Head will provide good practice. Midrange Seneca classics include *Breakneck* on the Cockscomb, a 5.4, so named because it was once done with a head jam (!), and *Conn's East*, an old Army route on the East Face, also a 5.4, which offers exposed climbing along a novel route to the South Peak summit. More difficult routes include *Thais Direct* (5.6) on the West Face, *Ecstasy* (a very nice 5.7 on the South End), and *Shipley's Shivering Shimmy (Triple-S)*, which is considered by many to be the classic Seneca route, a long 5.8 dihedral, done in one pitch, at the intersection of the Cockscomb and the Face of a Thousand Pitons.

More advanced routes can also be found on the Face of a Thousand Pitons. Next to *Triple-S* are *Agony* and *Marshall's Madness*, both 5.9, and just around the corner is the start of *Cottonmouth*, a 5.9 which can be done with a variation (called *Venom*) to make it a 5.10. Those looking for new route territory may find a place to squeeze in something new on the West Face below the North Peak, in the Pleasant Overhangs area below the South Peak, and on the Southern Pillar and some of the blank areas of the East Face, but the virgin territory is quickly vanishing. Other frontiers are still open, however, as a few of the aid routes are still waiting to be freed.

Visitors may be surprised to discover that rappelling is losing favor at Seneca. A rappelling death in recent years, as well as concern for the well-being of trees used as rappel anchors and a reluctance to be identified with individuals who visit the crags solely to rappel, have fostered a movement toward downclimbing the easier routes, such as *Old Ladies'* and *Old Man's*. Those who plan on rappelling to get off should make sure that they bring at least one, and preferably two, 150-foot ropes. The rappel routes are long and exposed.

Seneca is a pleasant place to climb, and the local climbers are doing everything possible to keep it that way. The vertically fractured structure of the rock make it unusual for the East, and it offers crack and face climbing

H. H. Heindel, Ohio climber-photographer, on the Tuscarora sandstone of Seneca Rock. (Photo by C. H. Burnett, courtesy H. H. Heindel)

of a type not found elsewhere east of the Mississippi. At present, there are no specific rules for climbing on Seneca, and the Forest Service has not shown signs of initiating any. The climbers in the area are very much in favor of the clean-climbing ethic, however, and pin and bolt use is almost obsolete on the rock, the necessary pitons being fixed on routes and maintained regularly. Seneca Rock is situated in a beautiful natural area—a fine place to climb in the footsteps of Princess Snowbird.

References

Hubbard, Donald. "DB Rediscovered." *Off Belay*, no. 26 (April 1976), pp. 23–24.

Jones, Chris. *Climbing in North America*. Berkeley: University of California Press for American Alpine Club, 1976. Pp. 180–82.

Owens, Don. Interview. August 1977.

Pleiss, Rich, and Webster, Bill. *Seneca Rocks, W. Va.; A Climber's Guide*. Montoursville, Pa.: Nippenose Books, 1976.

4

The Cathedral Spires
of the Needles

Mention the Black Hills and rock faces to just about anyone, and the first thing that comes to mind will probably be Mount Rushmore. Often, even well-traveled rock climbers will think of the area only in fantasies of doing the *Nose Route* on George Washington or of pulling the *Teddy Roosevelt Eyebrow Overhang*. Since a stiff fine and a possible jail sentence await anyone who attempts either of these climbs, the Black Hills region is often ignored by the climber as he speeds through it on his way to better-known climbing spots. This is something of a pity. The Black Hills are home to one of the most unusual, if little-known, rock climbing areas in the United States.

Custer State Park, near Hermosa, South Dakota, is an excellent example of Black Hills scenery at its best. The name Black Hills suggests to some people that the region is a stark and desolate place. The rich forests of the park prove that this is a misconception. Like the Black Forest, the Black Hills region earned its name because its vegetation appeared dark from a distance. But to the rock climber, the forest is just a scenic bonus in this area.

Nestled in the woodlands of Custer State Park are
hundreds of strange, rounded spires, like giant stalagmites
in search of a cave. These are the Needles of South
Dakota, eroded pinnacles of granite and pegmatite—a
veritable rock climber's playground.

The Needles managed to make it well into the 20th
century without causing much of a stir. When plans were
made to sculpt a huge stone memorial to four famous
American presidents, the Needles were the original site
considered for the great carving. Fortunately for the
climbing future of the area, the pegmatite and the irregu-
lar chimneys of the Needles formations made them unsuit-
able for sculpture, and nearby Mount Rushmore got the
facelifting instead.

In 1936, Fritz Weissner made the first recorded ascent
in the Needles, when he and his party climbed Inner
Outlet rock. On the ascent, they found evidence of an
earlier (but unrecorded) attempt. The next year, just
before making the first ascent of Devils Tower, Weissner
returned with Bill House and Larry Coveney to do more

Cathedral Spires in winter. (Courtesy Custer State Park)

new routes in the area as warm-ups for the Tower. Two of the more notable of these were the regular route up the East Face of Spire Two in the Cathedral Spires group, and an impressive 5.7 on Khayyam Spire, one of the most spectacular spires in the Cathedral group.

After these ascents, climbing in the Needles was dormant through the years of World War II, with nothing more interesting than a class 4 ascent of Loeber's Leap, a ridge summit, by two teenage girls from Lincoln, Nebraska. Then, after the war, a most unusual climbing boom took place at the Needles. Increased climbing activity was reported at almost every area in the country during the post–World War II years. Inexpensive Army-surplus equipment and an increased number of climbers due to the wartime training of mountain troops were the cause of much of this boom. What made the upswing of climbing in the Needles unique was that it was all due to the activity of just two climbers. Even stranger, these climbers were joined not only by the rope, but by matrimony. Their names were Herb and Jan Conn.

The Conns learned to climb in the Washington, D.C., area with friends from the National Bureau of Standards. One day, while glancing through a geography book, they found a picture of the Cathedral Spires. This whetted their appetites, and in 1947, while on a cross-country trip, they climbed in the Needles for the first time. During this trip, they made first ascents of the Fan (5.1) and Exclamation Point (5.3), two ridge summits descending from the Pinnacle known as Bloody Spire. Those two climbs were the beginning of a series of first ascents which Herb and Jan were to make over the next two decades. Their one-day stopover in 1947 generated enthusiasm for a week-long visit in 1948. After that trip, the Conns knew that they had found a home in the Needles. In 1949 they bought land to use as a campsite and as a possible lot for a home, and in 1951 they opened a mail-order leather goods business, built a home, and settled in the Black Hills for good.

Herb and Jan Conn then proceeded to weave themselves

Herb Conn and Jan Conn, climbing in the Needles. (Courtesy Herb and Jan Conn)

into the climbing history of the Black Hills. Herb realized a climber's fantasy by climbing on Mount Rushmore—in fact, he did it annually for a number of years as part of his job as a maintenance man for the memorial. Carrying a granite-colored crack filler, he would patch up small fissures and clean birds' nests from the presidential eyeballs. The Conns also made a name for themselves in area subterranean climbing, since they did the bulk of the exploring and mapping of Jewel Cave, the fourth largest cave in the world, which they discovered to be only 20 miles from their front door.

To rock climbers, however, the Conns' most significant achievement has been their climbing record in the Needles. Together, they have recorded well over 200 first ascents on the area's pegmatite summits.

It was only natural that Herb and Jan's favorite area in the Needles would be the Cathedral Spires group. The largest group in the Needles, the Cathedral Spires are the location of most of the longer climbs, and the group as a whole provides all the elements of enjoyable rock climbing—exposure, tricky moves, small but secure holds, route-finding problems, and a short approach walk. Noticing that the many spires of the Cathedral group fell into nine subgroups, each topped by a dominant spire, the Conns started systematically naming the pinnacles, with the largest spire in each subgroup getting the group number as a name, and recording their climbs. This activity eventually resulted in a mapping of the area by the pair, who even went so far as to make a perfect map—an exact miniature of the Cathedral Spires, sculpted in wax.

The Conns also established dozens of routes in the Cathedral Spires, covering a wide range of difficulty. They recall as among their favorites a 5.0 on the North Face of the Obelisk, good for beginners and climbers seeking relief from the summer sun, and two difficult and demanding lines on the South Tower and East Gruesome (the easternmost of the Gruesome Twosome), rated 5.7 and 5.8, respectively.

The Conns also include among their favorite Cathedral climbs a route which is one of the best-kept secrets in climbing, an ascent of Spire Three that they made in 1949. They call it the *Secret Route*, and they won't say exactly where it is! The Needles guidebook records it as a twisting and turning easy fifth-class climb. For those who wish to indulge in detective work, I give the route description as the Conns gave it to me, more detailed than the guidebook description, but equally mysterious: "A long route for the Needles, 700 feet of wandering around, working your way toward the summit of Spire Three up and down chinmeys, cracks, and nubble faces typical of all Needles climbing." In a way it is fitting that Herb and Jan Conn, who did more than anyone else to pioneer Needles climbing, should have a private climb known only to them—it is only a small reward for giving the Needles to American rock climbing.

Recalling their climbs and rope partners of the postwar

decades, the Conns remarked that the climbers of those years were more often academic than athletic. They climbed mostly in order to have an outdoors experience denied to the masses, continuing tradition begun in Europe in the 19th century. The Conns said then that they often wondered what would happen when a climber approached the rock with strength and technique as well as brains. In the '60s, they got their answer. His name was John Gill.

Gill was an accomplished gymnast as well as a climber, and he brought to climbing the gymnast's concern for grace, fluidity, strength, and efficient technique. He applied these standards in a form of climbing called bouldering, the practice of doing a climb to master a tricky and strenuous series of moves, rather than simply to gain a summit. Of necessity, this form of climbing is done on relatively low routes to minimize the consequences of a fall, since a bouldering route is usually not done successfully until it has been worked out in a progression of ever-larger attempts, each ending in a fall. Bouldering shifted the focus in climbing from danger to style and technique, and it heralded the dawn of a new age for rock climbing. Bouldering routes are now recognized as the most technically difficult rock climbs in the world, although most are done ropeless and are therefore third class.

Today, as a rock climber walks about the Cathedral Spires, the nearby Needle's Eye, Sylvan Lake, and other Needles areas, he may notice tiny arrows, about two inches long, pointing up short faces of rock. These arrows indicate bouldering routes pioneered by Gill and other boulderers, and they point out some of the most improbable-looking routes a climber could hope to find. To have climbed some of these routes is the hallmark of an accomplished climber.

Yet Gill did not, as many people suspect, have a built-in altitude limit of 20 feet, or a lead-climbing phobia. The Needles are sprinkled with his lead climbs, and routes such as his line on West Gruesome are mile-markers

Jan Conn, on lead in the Cathedral Spires. (Courtesy Herb and Jan Conn)

showing where he climbed with friends before going off on his own to establish standards which skyrocketed off the high end of the rating systems.

The rock climber stopping at the Needles today will have to do a bit of rethinking before tackling climbs of the grade to which he is accustomed. There is little, if any, rock in America quite like that of the pinnacles of Custer State Park. The surface of the rock teems with small crystals and is highly abrasive. This means that handholds, even when quite small, are generally usable and secure, but it also means that a fall can turn into quite a painful slide. This abrasiveness is quite apparent in chimneys, where the rock can quickly air-condition one's climbing pants unless only the hands and feet are used in climbing.

The rock is also remarkably free of cracks and fault lines. Because of this, a leader often will have to content himself with placing chocks between crystals or simply leading without protection. Piton use has declined in the area, and bolts are very much frowned upon. The summits are quite small in diameter (one often straddles them to belay), and wide use is made of a unique rappelling system in which the first climber rappels with a firmly seated partner who acts as a rappel anchor! The rope is then tied to a tree or some such point and laid over the summit, and the rest of the party raps down the other side. Visitors seeing this for the first time have been known to develop a new love for downclimbing.

The area spires are apt to be a bit confusing to the newcomer, since the spires all look something like large psychedelic anthills, and it is handy to have a good guidebook. (The current one is *A Climber's Guide to the Needles in the Black Hills of South Dakota*, by Bob Kamps.) Otherwise, the newcomer may be in for some confusion. When I first climbed the Needles, I jumped out of the car and onto the rock and, after a short period of traversing and climbing, descended to realize that I had no idea where I was. Fortunately, another hour of equally enjoyable climbing and a bit of blind luck reunited me with my companions.

The Cathedral Spires and the immediately surrounding areas are the most popular climbing areas in the Needles. The Needle's Eye area, not too far away, is also popular, but it is close to a road and parking area, so spectators are inevitable. At the Needle's Eye, a bulging pinnacle called the Sore Thumb is worth looking at.

A couple of decades ago, some collegiate climbers heard that the European Alps were often topped by crosses placed by first-ascent parties. They also heard that the

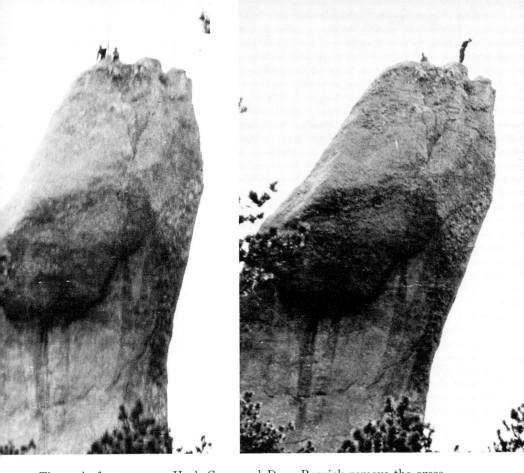

The end of an eyesore: Herb Conn and Dave Rearick remove the cross from the top of the Sore Thumb. (Courtesy Herb and Jan Conn)

Sore Thumb was supposed to be unclimbable, so with more enthusiasm than style they spent long hours putting a bolt ladder up the Thumb, after which they hauled up a six-foot fluorescent-orange cross made of steel tubing, and planted it on the top in a steel drum filled with rocks. After a couple of years, Herb Conn got tired of the eyesore, so he and Dave Rearick did a pendulumed aid route to the top (the first party had chopped all the bolts on the descent) and took down the cross, and the Sore Thumb stopped looking like the site of an H. P. Lovecraftian revival meeting.

Custer State Park has no regulations concerning climbing in the Needles, requesting only that reasonable care and common sense be exercised. So far, these have been all that is necessary in this most unusual climbing area. On trips cross-country which pass nearby, the Needles are certainly worth a stop.

References

Block, Ed. Review of *The Jewel Cave Adventure*. *Off Belay*, no. 34 (October 1973), p. 49.

Conn, Herb and Jan. Letter of December 1977.

Hamilton, Larry and Leslie. "Black Hills: A Photo Essay." *Climbing*, September/October 1975, pp. 18–19.

Kamps, Bob. *A Climber's Guide to the Needles in the Black Hills of South Dakota*. New York: American Alpine Club, 1971.

Smutek, Ray. "Pickin' Teddy's Nose." *Off Belay*, no. 11 (October 1972), p. 51.

5

Redgarden Wall
of Eldorado Springs Canyon

In the weird combinations of myth, boast, and tales of
horror which constitute the spoken histories of climbing,
there are some places whose mention must be followed
with a story. These places, whose climbs have a fable for
each crack and whose climbers are the subjects of a
thousand anecdotes, are the epicenters of a climbing
region, crucibles of modern climbing. One such place is
Eldorado Springs Canyon, near Boulder, Colorado.

In a state such as Colorado, where a climber can invest a
bare minimum of travel time and have his choice of
climbing alpine granite, desert sandstone, or canyon shale
and pegmatite, it is hard to visualize anything approaching a focal point for climbing. Yet, though it is true that
there are a few holdout specialists in the state who will not
stray from one area, it is remarkable to note that when
talking to climbers anywhere in Colorado, the visitor can
expect to hear, as the Spanish once heard, "golden tales of
Eldorado."

Perhaps history and population have much to do with
the interest in Eldorado. Boulder has long been popular

with climbers because of such outcrops as the Flatirons, and it has long been a training ground for the Colorado Mountain Club. Boulder is also located almost halfway between Denver, Colorado's largest city, and Rocky Mountain National Park, the state's most-visited recreational area. The climate of the Boulder area is milder than that of many other Colorado areas, and the area is in the vicinity of the state's largest freeway hub. Finally, situated as it is on the periphery between the eastern plains and the uplifted peneplain of the Rockies' Front Range, Boulder can be pictured as a gateway to the Colorado high country—a natural congregating site of climbers.

Yet Eldorado's reputation cannot be attributed merely to local preference or geographic situation. The climbing there has always been aesthetically pleasing, technically demanding, and hard on the frontiers of international climbing standards. I recall meeting a friend from the East, a Shawangunks local, on the flanks of Mount Lady Washington one morning. He mentioned that he had been to Eldorado, and when I, in the manner of climbers everywhere, began questioning him about the comparative difficulties of the routes and about his opinions of the area, he exclaimed, "I just couldn't believe it! Here I'd been climbing for years, secure in the knowledge that Western climbers overrate their routes, and I got out here and found out that it was all a lie! The stuff down in Eldorado is as hard as the Gunks, but it's different. I've been building up all this arm strength for doing overhangs out East, and I got out here, and it's useless! Just incredible. . . . "

In recent years, Eldorado Springs Canyon has started to attract climbers from all over the world, thus becoming the Rocky Mountains' counterpart of the Shawangunks and the Yosemite Valley. The Bastille, a principal face in the canyon, has been soloed, live, on national television, and Eldorado locals have gone on to become prominent in other regions, as was dramatically demonstrated by Steve Wunsch's *Supercrack*, on Mohonk in the Gunks, at this writing the hardest free climb in the country.

Given such attention by first-rate climbers, the routes on the sandstone of Eldorado Springs Canyon are many and difficult, with each rock and wall the central point of a unique facet of Colorado climbing history. However, at the head of a list of Eldorado principals, one would probably find a feature called Redgarden Wall.

Redgarden Wall was unclimbed until 1956, when Charles Murley, Cary Huston, Dallas Jackson, and Richard Bird pioneered the classic *Redguard Route* (5.7), a then difficult line up the right side of the wall. Opening the face to climbing at such a relatively late time was not unusual for an area with such an abundance of prospective routes. Yet, once completed, the *Redguard Route* announced that the wall was climbed and opened. The climbing response to this action has not slowed down yet.

Perhaps no subsequent climber of Redgarden Wall is as well known as the Boulder legend called Layton Kor. A bricklayer who was drawn to climbing by mountaineering stories and movies, Kor is the center of any number of Colorado climbing legends, most of which paint him as a character somewhere between the extremes of Laurel and

George Hurley leads the first pitch of the *Grand Giraffe*. (Photo by John Fort, courtesy George Hurley)

Hardy and Superman. His relationship to a route often bordered on masochism, and his seconds often recall Kor exclaiming over the horrible nature of a pitch just before recklessly hurling himself into it.

Layton, nicknamed "Hard Kor" by his climbing partner Pat Ament, was only learning to climb when the *Redguard Route* was first ascended. Yet by 1959 he had pioneered two routes on Redgarden Wall, *The Bulge* (5.7) and *T–2* (now free at 5.9). The latter was seconded by a youngster named Gerry Roach, who was something of a novice at the time. This, too, was to become a Kor tradition. Layton would run into raw, young climbers at bars, parties, and on the cliffs. He'd talk them into doing something "easy" over at Eldorado and then haul them, panic-stricken, up some horror show of a first ascent.

In 1960, with George Hurley (who knew Layton well enough to expect anything), Kor pioneered the *Grand Giraffe*, which, despite its tongue-in-cheek name, still has a reputation as one of the more serious routes on Redgarden. The third pitch involved an awkward crack to be done free at a rating of 5.9. The route became known as a testpiece, on a par with anything being climbed in America at the time.

During the '60s such names as Jack Turner, Steve Komito, Stanley Shepard, Larry Dalke, Pat Ament, and Bob Culp were also first heard around the Boulder area. Turner accompanied Kor on the first ascent of the *Rosicrucifixion* (5.9), and the two later rescued Ament and Dalke from the *Yellow Spur* (5.9) after a storm had snarled and frozen their ropes before they could complete a retreat to the canyon floor. Shepard was a sometime partner of Kor's and one of the canyon's top route engineers. Komito was a colorful touch of area wit, and Culp was one of the first soloists in the area. Komito and Culp went on to make their living in climbing, Komito as one of the finest boot makers in the world and Culp as the owner of the highly respected Bob Culp Climbing School, which is directed by George Hurley.

Bob Culp on lead on the steep
and exposed *Rosicrucifixion*.
(Photo by Bob Godfrey)

During the '70s, Eldorado, and particularly Redgarden Wall, continued to excite activity in the front waves of international rock climbing. Exposure to Yosemite Valley climbing techniques and East Coast philosophies produced a channeling effect on the climbers of the Eldorado area, with an emphasis on clean climbing and the total elimination of aid. The leading climbers included Bill Briggs, Dudley Chelton, Duncan Ferguson, Jim Erickson, Steve Wunsch, and a host of others. An Eldorado climber named Diana Hunter proved that women could climb at the upper extremes just as competently as men, employing a dancer's grace to overcome crux moves usually done with brute force and opening a path for a legion of fine female climbers throughout the country. Sadly, Diana also became the first high-standard climber of her sex to die in a climbing accident, when a handhold gave way during an unroped climb in 1975. The growing number of women climbing at or beyond the 5.10 level is mute testimony to her pioneer courage and vision.

An example of the evolution of rock climbing on Red-

garden Wall can be seen in the route called *Kloeberdanz*.
With Bob Culp, Layton Kor first attempted this line in the
dawn of the '60s. It involved climbing a steep face, over-
coming an awkwardly angled roof, and traversing and
climbing the steep and delicate ground beyond. Kor's
casual approach to the roof, improvising a poorly placed
pin as a handhold, came apart when the handhold did,
quickly ending the first attempt.

Kloeberdanz was successfully climbed by Kor in 1962,
when he returned with Larry Dalke and a proper inven-
tory of direct aid equipment. The roof fell easily enough,
but the traverse just beyond and the line above were
extremely dicey, and they rated the nailing A4. On a
repeat of the route in 1965, Dalke, unable to see how Kor
had aided the pitch above the roof, led it free, at 5.9. He
knew how to nail the roof, and with the relative lack of

George Hurley climbing in Eldorado Springs Canyon. Hurley has been
a leading Eldorado climber for more than a decade and is now
administrator for the Bob Culp School. (Photo by Bob Bliss, courtesy
Bob Culp School)

emphasis on free climbing in the mid-60s, it was gladly passed with aid.

As the decade closed and the more obvious lines were conquered in the canyon, the attention of the climbing community was focused on freeing the old aid routes. *Kloeberdanz* was a prime target, and a variety of people spent summer days falling off its roof. Finally, in 1973, Steve Wunsch and Jim Erickson devoted numerous falls to figuring out a series of dynamic swings to the edge of the roof, followed by what is best described as a prehensile heel move, over the edge of the roof. This dynamic free technique moved to obsolescence when a teenage boulder specialist named David Breashears climbed the roof conventionally, without a single dynamic swing.

Even at this point, the evolution was not yet complete. Once *Kloebardanz* had been statically led and protected cleanly at a rating of 5.11, the next move was to redefine aid and eliminate anything that would fall into that category. To the Eldorado climbers, this meant using a protection point both as a resting place and for climbing. Leading on a slack rope became necessary for good style. Then a climber named Pat Adams brought this ethic to its logical conclusion by climbing *Kloeberdanz* unroped and without protection. This eliminated even the possibility of using aid, and, ironically enough, it reduced the rating of the climb to class 3!

The limits, however, have not been reached yet. The use of gymnast's chalk in free climbing has been challenged by leading Eldorado climbers on the grounds of both technique and aesthetics. The use of chemicals to toughen the fingertips is also considered questionable, and in the future there will no doubt be a school of climbers who will frown on the wearing of friction boots in free ascents. If there is an upper limit to this evolution of rock climbing, it is cloud-shrouded and hidden.

The climber who wishes to visit Eldorado and climb Redgarden Wall will find both *Eldorado*, by Pat Ament, and *High over Boulder*, by Cleve McCarty and Pat Ament,

George Hurley leads out on the West Buttress of the Bastille. (Photos by Bob Bliss, courtesy Bob Culp School)

to be useful guides. Up-to-date information and equipment is obtainable at The Boulder Mountaineer, at Broadway and University Avenue in Boulder. This is also the location of Bob Culp's climbing school, which can provide the visitor with climbing lessons or offer daily or half-day guide service to Eldorado climbs, with some of the area's most outstanding climbers as guides.

Like the Shawangunks, Eldorado Springs Canyon is privately owned, and a fee must be paid for access to the canyon. However, the resort owners who hold the deed to the canyon land have expressed a desire to sell it. An offer to sell the land as a park to the city of Boulder did not result in purchase, and the owners have been looking

elsewhere for buyers. As of this writing, two parties are investigating the possibilities of buying Eldorado—the state of Colorado and a local quarrying firm which wishes to use the canyon as a source of gravel.

Climbers throughout the nation have taken action to prevent the reduction of Redgarden Wall to so many acres of driveway topping. They are making efforts to persuade Colorado legislators that the area deserves preservation as a park, and they are collecting funds that will be donated to the state to help purchase the canyon. At the moment, the state is conducting feasibility studies concerning a canyon park, but building in the Denver strip has also increased the area demand for gravel, and the owner, who holds the canyon as a real estate investment, is rightly enough looking for a fair return on his property. Perhaps by the time this book is published the question of Eldorado Springs Canyon's future will have been resolved. One can only hope that the solution will be compatible with the area's rich climbing history.

References

Ament, Pat. "Bouldering around Boulder." *Climbing*, September 1970, pp. 19–21.

Ament, Pat. "Portrait of the Yellow Spur." *Climbing*, May/June 1976, pp. 6–7.

"The Bob Culp Climbing School" (advertising brochure).

Briggs, Roger. "Reflections on Recent Climbing in Boulder." *Climbing*, Winter 1973–74, pp. 6–11.

Chelton, Dudley, and Godfrey, Bob. *Climb!* Boulder, Colo.: Alpine House for American Alpine Club, 1977. Pp. 78, 81, 98, 112–13, 152–55, 181, 203–08, and 219.

Covington, Mike. "Boulder Area." *Mountain*, no. 39 (October 1974), pp. 9–10.

Erickson, Jim. "El Dorado Threatened" (letter). *Mountain*, no. 41 (January 1975), pp. 40–41.

Erickson, Jim, and Wunsch, Steve. "The Future of Eldorado Springs Canyon" (letter). *Mountain*, no. 49 (May/June 1976), pp. 42–43.

Hurley, George. Telephone interview. December 1977.

Marquardt, Larry. "Eldorado Alternatives." *Climbing*, March/April 1976, pp. 13–17.

Owens, Don. Interview. January 1978.

Webster, Ed. "Boulder Area." *North American Climber*, November 1975, pp. 9–10.

Wunsch, Steve. "Kloeberdanz: A Free Ascent." *Climbing*, May/June 1974, pp. 6–10.

Part 2
Classics

Word association tells one a lot about a person. For example, the word *mountain* may evoke any number of replies. "Climb," "high," and "powerful" are among the abstract responses to this word, but with a climber it is probable that the first response will be a mental image of one particular peak that summarizes all that the climber associates with the idea "mountain." To a Swiss climber it probably would be the Matterhorn; a Mexican mountaineer might picture Popocatepetl; a Canadian mountaineer, Mount Assiniboine or Mount Robson; and an African climber would probably form an image of Kilimanjaro. To the Japanese climber, it would be Fujiyama; to the Russian climber, Mount Communism or Tengri Khan. To many climbers everywhere, it would be Mount Everest.

These peaks all have one thing in common—they are classics in every sense of the word. To those who are familiar with them, the classic peaks symbolize all that there is to know about mountaineering. A classic peak may be a volcanic cone or a granite alp, a gentle walk-up steeped in history, or a gigantic fang that resists all attempts at conquest. Nonetheless, to those who know the peak, it is *the* mountain.

America's abundance of mountains has generated a host of classics. In every corner of the country, distinctive peaks and their reputations tell volumes about the climbers who frequent them. Often these peaks are the centers of long and colorful climbing histories, and just as often they are the springboards to new horizons of climbing. These peaks have been known by generations and have stood the test of time. To pass that test, to stand good and whole despite the passage of time, is the truest sign of a classic.

It is the nature of the mountaineer to roam. He is a being who constantly yearns for new horizons, departs for distant lands, climbs new routes, and reaches new summits. But between the next climb and the last, when the man without returns home before venturing abroad again, the man within returns to the classic peaks. Inhospitable to his body, they are home to his soul.

6

Mount Washington

To the Western mountaineer who has traveled the high country of the Sierra Nevada, the Front Range, the Olympics, Wind Rivers, or the Cascades, the very idea of "Mount" Washington may seem to be Eastern exaggeration. And at first glance Mount Washington seems to support the Westerner's point of view. Rising to only 6,288 feet above the Atlantic, Washington would rank in many Western ranges as a hill, and a very civilized hill indeed. The summit, now a New Hampshire state park, is available to mechanized mountaineers by toll road or rail, with horse trails and maintained paths to the top for those who prefer to rough it. Once at the top, the Mount Washington climber would do well to be prepared for some company. The summit is occupied by, among other things, an observatory, a radio station, a television station, and a museum, and once it even had its own newspaper.

All of this would convince most hikers and climbers that Mount Washington is a joke, a mere lark to be taken any way but seriously. It is just such an attitude that has cost more than 60 people their lives in attempts to climb it.

Mount Washington. (Photo by Pat Bessner)

Like the pleasantly furry animal that greets the unwary with a venomous bite, Mount Washington is a gamble with death for those unprepared to deal with its darker side.

Washington, the highest peak in New Hampshire's Presidential Range, is named after this country's first president, and in many ways it is the nation's first mountain. It was sighted from the Atlantic as early as 15 years before the founding of Jamestown, and its first recorded ascent took place in June 1642, when an Exeter resident named Darby Field led a climb of what he knew as Christall Hill in search of valuable ores and diamonds. Finding only quartz, Field and his companions left, leaving the mountain to the various Indian tribes of the region, who called it Agiochook, "The Mountain With Snow on Its Head."

With stories of treasure firmly dispelled, Agiochook lost the interest of the layman and attracted only academicians. A 1784 expedition, interested in botany and geography, became the first party to camp on the summit and gave the peak its present name. In the next few years,

Mount Washington's cog railway turns mountaineering into a true leisure sport. (Photo by Pat Bessner)

Mount Washington was visited by scientists representing the various branches of biology and geology.

By 1819, the Northeast had become established enough to warrant a recreation center. With the Indians of the area firmly routed to points west, Abel Crawford and his son, Ethan, opened an inn on Mount Washington's western side and built the first trail to the summit. The Crawfords were amiable guides, sometimes carrying their clients to the top, but this function became unnecessary when Ethan opened a bridle path to the top in 1840.

In 1869, the installation of a railway made it possible for a traveler to go to the top of Mount Washington with no more exertion than it took to step into a railway carriage. Nor was the railway the only addition to the landscape. Other businessmen began helping themselves to slices of the Crawfords' pie. In 1851 a hotel, complete with its own bridle path to the summit, was built at Pinkham Notch, and within the next two years two lodging houses appeared on the mountain top. Another mode of transportation opened in 1861, when a carriage road was built from

Pinkham Notch to the top. In 1871, a railway depot was opened at the summit.

The summit grew into a small village, but in July 1908 most of the summit buildings, including a new hotel, burned to the ground. The rebuilt summit complex was a bit less tourist-oriented, and today the installations at the summit are primarily concerned with airwave communication and scientific observation.

The dangerous aspect of this civilized little mountain has much to do with its location and the placement of surrounding peaks. Mount Washington lies in a major storm path. The mountains around it serve as funnels and airfoils which channel even more bad weather its way. High winds, violent storms, sudden whiteouts, and drastic drops in temperature are all part of the normal Mount Washington weather pattern. It is safe to say that this mountain has some of the worst weather in the world.

The summit complex on Mount Washington. (Photo by Dick Smith, courtesy state of New Hampshire)

High winds and supercooled droplets coat Mount Washington's summit with rime during much of the year. (Photos by Dick Smith, courtesy state of New Hampshire)

Winds, for example, have been clocked over the summit at more than 100 miles per hour for extended periods of time. A world-record gust in 1934 pushed the needle well past 230 miles per hour before blowing the measuring device away. It is not uncommon for such winds to be laden with supercooled moisture droplets, which quickly plaster any exposed object and encase it in thick layers of rime. More than 550 inches of snow have fallen on Mount Washington in a single year, and almost 50 inches of new snowfall have been measured in one day.

Even the summertime temperature on the summit is rarely above 70 degrees, and winter temperatures dropping to −46° F are not unheard of. When temperatures like these are combined with winds gusting from near-calm conditions to well above 100 miles per hour, it is ridiculous even to consider windchill factors. Simply stated, the mountain's weather can be lethal at times to anyone caught in the open.

Summer hazards include unexpected storms of surprising intensity and large drops in temperature, with a corresponding danger of hypothermia to the unprepared traveler. At any time of year, the climber or hiker who attempts this mountain without fully understanding and preparing for the truly awesome weather Mount Washington has to offer is laying his life on the line. It is not a mountain to be taken lightly.

In 1849, Frederick Strickland, an English visitor, became disoriented in an autumn storm on Mount Washington and became the first unprepared hiker to die on its slopes. It is sad to note that dozens of hikers have since perished in the same way and that almost all of the deaths were partly due to a lack of preparation. Warm clothing, windproof and waterproof coverings, and the ability to recognize hypothermia before rewarming becomes impossible are three keys which can save a Mount Washington visitor from an early grave. A fourth is common sense—

which is perhaps more difficult to acquire than any of the other keys.

With proper foresight, Mount Washington can change from a terrifying death trap to an enjoyable ascent on a number of fronts. The Appalachian Mountain Club, the U.S. Forest Service, and the Randolph Mountain Club all maintain trails which provide a pleasant mountain experience for more than 50,000 people each year, although the trail hiking can vary with the weather from a balmy afternoon's stroll to a tooth-numbing alpine classic. Mount Washington also has something to offer the technical climber. Glacial cirques, such as Tuckerman Ravine, Huntington Ravine, and the Great Gulf, offer numerous rock climbing possibilities. Huntington Ravine is famous for long, exposed rock climbs as well as some of the finest mixed snow and ice climbing in New England. Winter mixed climbing is popular in the Tuckerman area, with spring being the preferred season for ice climbing. Spring is also a time when the local extreme skiers appear at Tuckerman Ravine, however, and ice climbers will do well to make sure that they are not cramponing up someone's fall line.

It is wise to advise someone of your plans to climb or hike on Mount Washington, and a good place to do this is at the Appalachian Mountain Club Base Camp in Pinkham Notch. The AMC also operates a series of porter-provisioned huts in the area, a nice alternative to carrying one's camp while hiking in the Presidentials. Preclimb or prehike registration is of inestimable importance. Whether an effort to locate an overdue hiker is a rescue party or a body search depends largely on the timeliness of the effort, and registering before leaving does much toward ensuring that the effort will not be a body search.

With its objective dangers carefully weighed, Mount Washington can be a useful training ground for groups preparing for Arctic climbing. It is conveniently close to large population centers, while offering weather conditions rarely if ever encountered below the Arctic Circle.

References

Bueler, William A. *Mountains of the World*. Rutland Vt.: Charles E. Tuttle Co., 1970. P. 18.

Gerath, Robert F. "Mount Washington and the Presidential Range." *Summit*, December 1969, pp. 2–9.

Gosselin, Guy. "New Hampshire's Mount Washington." *Backpacker*, no. 17 (October 1976), pp. 26–30+.

McMorrin, Ian, and Noyce, Wilfred. *World Atlas of Mountaineering*. London: Thomas Nelson and Sons, 1969. P. 166.

Rubin, Al. "The New England Winter." *Mountain*, no. 21 (May 1972), pp. 22, 26–27.

7

Hallet Peak

For many climbers, Rocky Mountain National Park is synonymous with Western mountaineering. And for many of the climbers who hold this view, Long's Peak is the mountain associated with the park. Yet even a casual glance around Estes Park, Colorado, will convince anyone that Long's Peak is not the only mountain around.

The mixture of climbs on Long's, its magnetism for tourists, and its status as the highest peak in Rocky Mountain National Park all help to account for the fact that one peak bears more than 60 percent of the park's climbing traffic. Obviously, this leaves a lot of room in the park to beat the crowds.

Hallet Peak is a fine example of a Rocky Mountain alternative. At 12,713 feet, it does not have the altitude of Long's, but to those who climb for more than rarefied atmosphere, Hallet can be a very satisfying choice. It has the ingredients of a good mountain—challenge, variety, and an aura of history.

No one knows who made the first ascent of Hallet Peak. Frederick Chapin reached its top in 1887, but a cairn on the summit advertised the previous ascent of some unknown trapper or surveyor, giving Chapin the secondhand privilege of having made the first recorded ascent. Yet even the cairn builder was probably preceded in his climb. The Ute Indians used many of the high peaks in the area as lookout posts and as trapping sites on which to capture eagles. It is very probable that Hallet was first climbed by the Ute, giving the distinction of its first ascent to a Native American.

Most of the people who visit the summit of Hallet each year do so by walking or riding to the top. As is typical of the peaks in Rocky Mountain National Park, Hallet has an easy side. From the Bear Lake ranger station, only horse or boot power are needed to take the Flattop Mountain Trail to the summit of Flattop, after which a bit more than a half-mile of scrambling will put the climber past the head of the Tyndall Glacier and onto the highest portion of Hallet's rounded summit. For those who desire more than this scenic but easy ridge route, the North Face will probably fill the bill.

The North Face has been the site of the bulk of Hallet Peak's technical climbing history. Approximately 800 feet high, this long glacially formed wall of granite schist offers the climber anything from a Grade I 5.0 to a Grade III 5.8 or 5.7 A1.

The North Face of Hallet is divided into three faces called the First, Second, and Third buttresses. Between the First Buttress and the Second Buttress is a great dividing crack called *Hallet Chimney*. This is believed to be the side of the first technical ascent of the North Face, by Milton Wiley sometime after World War II. Like most north-facing chimneys in the area, this route (a 5.5) holds ice and seeps meltwater until the late summer months. In his guidebook, Walt Fricke mentions a party in the '50s that received a rather gruesome surprise when it topped one of the route's chockstones to find the body of a tourist who had fallen from the ridge above.

An easier, and often drier, route in the general vicinity

Hallet Peak, Rocky Mountain National Park, in winter. (Photo by Cecil W. Stoughton, courtesy National Park Service)

is the *First Buttress Route*, a Grade I 5.4 to the left of *Hallet Chimney*. Although not as direct as the chimney, this route is wide open to invention, being third and fourth class much of the way, with the technical portion at the top. All things considered, it is a pleasant introduction to climbing on the Hallet buttresses.

The Hallet classic, however, is the *Northcutt-Carter Route* on the steep Third Buttress. In 1956, when the buttress was still virgin territory, a pair of former mountain troopers named Ray Northcutt and Harvey Carter began to study the possibilities of the face. At the time there were no high-standard technical routes on the steep faces of the park peaks, and the pair were fully aware that they were breaking new ground.

Northcutt and Carter took the climb quite seriously, and devoted long hours of physical conditioning to preparation for the climb. Even then, a combination of difficult route finding and hard climbing brought their first effort to a halt a little more than halfway up the more-than-800-foot face.

On a later return, the pair used their advantage of previous experience on the face to pull off the climb in one long day. The resulting route, which dealt subsequently with face climbing, hand traverses, chimneys, corners, and overhangs, was a cause for much elation. *Northcutt-Carter* brought large-scale face climbing to the Rocky Mountain National Park area, and was an accomplishment unparalleled in the region.

Yet, though the climb may have been great shakes for the immediate area, its status nationally was quite another thing. One of the more often-repeated anecdotes about Colorado climbing is the story of Yvon Chouinard's and Ken Weeks's ascent of the Third Buttress.

This pair, who had honed their skills on Yosemite Valley granite and climbed throughout the United States, had heard tales and read stories about the incredibly difficult route on Hallet Peak. When they arrived, a reconnaissance seemed in order, and they set off late in the afternoon to try a few pitches and see what the rock was like. The going was relatively easy, so they kept climbing to try to find the hard part. They were still looking when they topped out on the climb four hours later.

In this view of Hallet Peak, the First Buttress is in sunlight and shadow to the left, the Second Buttress lies mostly in sunlight in the center, and the celebrated Third Buttress lies in shadow to the right. The *Northcutt-Carter Route* starts at the base of the Third Buttress directly below the summit prow; it finishes in the sunlit patch just to the left of the prow. (Courtesy National Park Service)

There is a difference between an alpine face and a big wall, as Chouinard and Weeks so eloquently proved. So did Layton Kor, who climbed the route in all seasons, and soloed it in an hour and a half. It is also worth noting that the Yosemite climbers took a more direct route than did the Coloradans, resulting in a line that was slightly more difficult, yet aesthetically more pleasing.

Yet, differences in local standards cannot change the fact that the route climbed by Northcutt and Carter was a milestone for Colorado and Rocky Mountain climbing. In an area where many peaks were customarily climbed by easy technical lines and dog routes, an attempt on a large face was a leap into new areas of climbing. Northcutt's and Carter's efforts opened interest in further climbing on the Hallet buttresses and led to other steep-face ascents, culminating in the first efforts on the Diamond, the major wall high on the East Face of Long's Peak.

Today, despite its historical significance and its challenging nature, Hallet Peak receives less than 2 percent of the Rocky Mountain National Park's climbing traffic. The peak is, however, easy to approach, climbable on almost any level of difficulty, in pleasant surroundings, and still open for new routes.

Climbing on Hallet is regulated by the same rules which apply to all technical climbing in Rocky Mountain National Park. These rules include the mandatory registration of all climbs and camping or bivouacking by permit only. Climbing permits are generally provided upon request, and bivouac permits are provided if the backcountry rangers think that a prospective route warrants a bivouac. In summer, one can register for a climb up to three days in advance, but in winter a day-before-the-trip climb registration is necessary. Only climbers can bivouac, and environmental protection is emphasized in the use of the park mountains and the backcountry.

A very good guide to the area is Walt Fricke's *A Climber's Guide to the Rocky Mountain National Park Area,* and the nearby town of Estes Park has a number of shops selling climbing equipment and lightweight camping gear. Of particular interest to climbers is Steve Komito's boot shop, which also houses Banana Equipment and the Fantasy Ridge School of Alpinism. Fantasy Ridge offers a guide service to the area under the direction of Michael Covington, and Komito's and Banana are good places to fill out thin spots in equipment and get up-to-date information.

Enjoyable to climb and important to the history of climbing, Hallet offers the climber route-finding problems, high-mountain atmosphere, and a retreat from the crowds. It is proof to the unbelieving that Long's is not the only peak in town.

References

Bueler, William M. *Roof of the Rockies*. Boulder, Colo.: Pruett Publishing Co., 1974. Pp. 98–99.

Chelton, Dudley, and Godfrey, Bob. *Climb!* Boulder, Colo.: Alpine House for American Alpine Club, 1977. Pp. 2, 82–84, and 233.

Fricke, Walter W., Jr. *A Climber's Guide to the Rocky Mountain National Park Area*. Boulder, Colo: Walter W. Fricke, Jr., 1971. Pp. 133–43.

Fricke, Walter W., Jr. "Climbing at Rocky Mountain." *Off Belay*, no. 2 (April 1972), pp. 17–23.

Hurley, George. Letter of December 1977.

Jones, Chris. *Climbing in North America*. Berkeley: University of California Press for American Alpine Club, 1976. Pp. 222, 290.

Anonymous. "More on National Parks." *Off Belay*, no. 21 (June 1975), pp. 39–41.

Anonymous. "National Parks Take Brunt of Mountaineering Traffic." *Off Belay*, no. 14 (April 1974), pp. 33–35.

Rocky Mountain National Park. "Technical Climbing and Bivouac Use" (regulations brochure).

8

Gannett Peak

Gannett Peak, named for Henry Gannett, a Rocky Mountain explorer and geologist, is known more for its character than for its characteristics. At 13,785 feet, it is the highest peak in Wyoming, topping the Grand Teton by almost 20 feet, and it is an attractive mixed climb, involving both rock and snow work. But mountaineers are more enticed by the aura of Gannett than by these features. Gannett Peak is the crowning summit of the Wind River Range, one of the most attractive mountain ranges in the United States.

The Winds, as many climbers call the range, are not one of the better known American mountain ranges, the name of the range being relatively foreign to the general public. Part of the reason for this is that it is not a prestige range. None of the summits push past the apparently magical 14,000-foot elevation. Nor does the range rise as steeply from the nearest flatlands as does, say, the Front Range. Moreover, the Wind River Range is not a range of peaks that one simply jumps out of the car and does. The range is miles from the nearest road—Gannett is about 28 miles

Gannett Peak, the highest point in Wyoming, and the Wind River Range. (Photo by Chuck Winger)

from the nearest highway—and the approach to the peaks is good, solid hiking, with many passes to cross and subsequent gains and losses of altitude. Since all of this tends to put the Winds slightly beyond the reach of the type of tourist who is more accustomed to ascending mountains by cable car than by crampons, "out of sight, out of mind" has kept the range rather low key. As a result, Gannett Peak and its neighbors have been left to the hardy hikers and mountaineers and have quietly served as the setting for many years of wilderness experience.

The first ascent of Gannett, which would also be the first ascent to the summit of the range, is a subject of some dispute. Many historians attribute it to a Captain Benjamin Bonneville, an early explorer of the area who was interested in finding a way *through* the mountains rather than a way *up* the mountains.

Feeling that it would be easier to diagnose their maze from above than from within, Bonneville and his companions climbed one of the smaller peaks in the Wind River

The Petzoldt Pinnacles, Glacier Pass, and Gannett Peak from a skyline in the Wind Rivers. The usual route skirts the glacier to the Gannett side of Glacier Pass and follows the skyline to the top. (Photo by Chuck Winger)

Range. Finding their view no less obscured, they then set off for a loftier survey point. They made a strenuous climb to a snow-covered summit, from which they were able to obtain a view of the entire Wind River Range and the lands beyond, clearly distinguishing the Grand Teton and its satellites. After examining the panorama in all directions, Bonneville decided that he was standing on the highest peak in the area, adding, for good measure, that he believed it to be the highest mountain on the continent.

There has been some hesitancy about crediting Bonneville with the first ascent of Gannett Peak. The main reasons for this hesitancy are that Bonneville reported fairly large vegetation well up on the peak, whereas the timberline in the area is only a bit above 10,500 feet, and that it is doubted whether his party had sufficient skill to make the climb, since the only prior ascent of a major Western mountain was that of Pikes Peak in 1820. Yet Bonneville's descriptions of the summit and his feeling

A mountaineer, his heavy pack and camp gear left behind to be picked up on his return, ascends a Gannett Peak snowfield. (Photo by Chuck Winger)

that he was on the highest peak in the region would seem to support the theory that he climbed Gannett. Clearly, this is a case for the arbitrators, though giving Bonneville credit for the ascent makes for colorful history, if nothing else.

Bonneville's story of his climb in the Wind River Range only added to the mystery of the mountains of the American West. Seen both as storehouses of limitless quantities of gold and precious stones and as impregnable fortresses blocking the way to the Pacific Coast, the Western mountains were to remain an enigma for some years to come. Indeed, at the very time that Bonneville felt that he was on the highest peak of the continent, the peak elevation of the Rockies was estimated at 25,000 feet! Those were very much frontier times.

Gannett and the Wind River Range have become better known and better loved. Gannett is a favorite objective of outing clubs and wilderness schools, and for many climbers it is an introduction to mountaineering. After disagreeing with his companions as to the proper route to take, Yvon Chouinard went off by himself to solo a new route on the west face. Incredibly enough, he lived through the experience and became one of the top all-around climbers in the world.

Taking such chances is, of course, not recommended. Sections of even the easier routes are fifth class, albeit lower fifth class, and broken faces and snowfields increase the possibility of danger. Furthermore, the weather in the area can change with alarming rapidity and can catch climbers on the northeast (lee) side quite unawares. For these reasons, as well as the isolation of the peak, it is a good idea to be with a group, to carry foul-weather gear and rock and snow equipment, and to study the route well in advance both in order to conserve time and to be prepared with a retreat route.

Travel in the Wind River Range involves many possible combinations of passage over the Bridger Wilderness Area, the Pope Agie and Glacier primitive areas, and the Wind River Indian Reservation, so it is wise to check carefully to be sure that the trails one will take are in compliance with area regulations. In particular, unauthorized travel over Indian land is very heavily frowned upon. It should also be noted that primitive areas should be kept that way. This means that stoves are to be used for cooking and that plants and materials found at campsites are to be left undisturbed.

Gannett Peak is approached by using either the Ink Wells Trail or the Glacier Trail, both of which are found at the end of secondary roads from U.S. 287. The Ink Wells Trail is shorter, but Indian permission is necessary to reach the trailhead from U.S. 287. From the end of these trails, at Wilson Meadows, Gannett is apparent as a peak with a large and long snowcapped summit. To its left is the obvious Gooseneck Pinnacle. Then, the Petzoldt Pinnacles are on a descending ridge. These pinnacles

The summit of Gannett Peak. Nearby, a summit register is kept in an iron pipe. (Photo by Chuck Winger)

ultimately lead back up to Mount Warren, which is only 65 feet lower than Gannett.

From Wilson Meadows, the usual route goes up the Dinwoody Glacier, at least one portion of which is usually heavily crevassed, and then past a slight step (a good resting spot) up the Gooseneck Glacier, making a right turn before the Gooseneck Pinnacle to gain the long summit ridge. The top affords a beautiful view on good days, and in fair weather one can see the Tetons, as Bonneville reported, 160 miles away.

Gannett Peak and the Winds River Range are an excellent choice for an off-the-beaten-path mountaineering trip. The approach to Gannett is long, but exceedingly pretty. Common sense demands that the approach be cut into two days, and aesthetic pleasures and frequent camera stops may lengthen this to three. Rain can be expected at some point in any trip in the area, and an ice ax should be in each member's equipment list for any season. Winter climbs will require a full array of alpine snow gear. Prepared for sensibly, the isolation of Gannett Peak adds nicely to one's enjoyment of the climb.

References

Bernstein, Jeremy. "Profiles: Ascending." *New Yorker*, 31 January 1978, pp. 37–53.

Bueler, William M. *Mountains of the World*. Rutland, Vt.: Charles E. Tuttle Co., 1970. Pp. 38–41.

Bueler, William M. *Roof of the Rockies*. Boulder, Colo.: Pruett Publishing Co., 1974. P. 48.

Bueler, William M. "What Did Bonneville Climb?" *Off Belay*, no. 24 (December 1975), pp. 7–9.

Cushman, Ruth Carol. "The Wind Rivers: Misty Mountains of Wyoming." *Summit*, August 1976, pp. 18–25.

Daley, Edward J. "Gannett Peak." *Summit*, November/December 1972, pp. 35–37.

Irving, Washington. "Wind Rivers 1833." *Off Belay*, no. 24 (December 1975), pp. 4–6.

Jones, Chris. *Climbing in North America*. Berkeley: University of California Press for American Alpine Club, 1976. Pp. 7–8.

McMorrin, Ian, and Noyce, Wilfred. *World Atlas of Mountaineering*. London: Thomas Nelson and Sons, 1969. Pp. 167–68.

Winger, Chuck. Interview. January 1978.

9

The Grand Teton

Mountaineers have special feelings for special peaks. Most climbers feel awe for Mount McKinley, whereas a lower but more angular mountain, such as Mount Robson, may generate mixed feelings of caution and pensiveness. Some mountains, such as Long's Peak, may create two conflicting emotions—gentleness and a fierce aloofness. For the Grand Teton, what many American climbers feel is mostly a moving fondness, for "the Grand," as climbers call it, is probably *the* American mountain.

The Grand Teton and the surrounding Teton Range are curious in that they have no foothills whatsoever. The range is just there, as if some cosmic magician had said the magic words and caused it to pop up out of the surrounding landscape. In a way, that is exactly what happened.

Unlike mountain ranges that were formed by great wrinkles on the earth's surface, the Tetons are examples of fault-block topography. The material of the range is from a variety of geologic sources, mostly igneous, and from a variety of geologic ages, with the oldest rock in the range

The Teton Range and Jackson Lake. (Photo by Steve Ranck)

dating well back beyond the 2,500-million-year mark. Like most igneous rock, this older material cracked and was later invaded by new igneous material, forming dikes of various hardnesses. The older rock in the range is generally a form of granite, whereas the dike material is generally a type of basalt. On top of this igneous material, sedimentary rock layers were formed, with limestone, sandstone, and shale predominating, and some traces of volcanic material can be found in the range as well.

All of this material was transformed into mountain range when pressures within the earth caused a shifting of landmasses. The earth was torn along a line now known as the Teton Fault, and a highly localized block was pushed skyward. A secondary fault was created to the west, as the landmass separated on that side as well, while to the east, on the other side of the Teton Fault, a corresponding depression of the landscape took place. On what had been fairly level ground, then, there were now three general changes: the primary block had been raised and pushed several thousand feet above its previous level to form the Teton Range; a tilting table of land was now to the west of the block; and to the east of the block, a broad valley—the Jackson Hole of today—stood at the very foot of the new range.

A fault-block mountain range, the Tetons rise dramatically from the flatlands to the east. (Photo by Pat Bessner)

Even as the slow fault-block process was shoving the Tetons skyward, another geologic event, the Great Ice Age, was taking place. The Teton snowfields became glaciers, and these glaciers wound their way down toward Jackson Hole, scooping depressions to form the lakes of later times, and gouging out the broad valleys of the present range, removing most sedimentary material from its once-flat top, and dumping this matter into the Jackson Hole valley.

Evidence of glacial action includes the sculpting of the actual Tetons and the moraine (ridge) and outwash plain geography in the Jackson Hole area. Further evidence is provided by large depressions in the earth, called kettles, which indicate spots where gigantic chunks of ice were once buried in the glacial plain. When those chunks melted, the earth sank, creating the kettles.

Generally, evidence of block faulting and glacial action is not extraordinary, but the Teton Range and the surrounding area are a highly compact example of those forces. This is why many high school and college students first meet the Tetons through maps and texts in geography classes.

But the Tetons are not only educational. They are also beautiful, the answer to a postcard photographer's prayers. Non-Indians first saw their beauty in the very early

years of the 19th century. In 1811, the three Tetons were
sighted by Wilson Hunt, leader of an expedition for the
Astor Fur Company, who assigned them the unimagina-
tive name Pilot Knobs. This lack of imagination was
emended seven years later, when some French trappers
with the Stuart party named the peaks Les Trois Tetons.
Millions of visitors view the Grand Teton each year,
unaware of the French origin of its name. If they only
knew, many of these honorable citizens would be shocked
to hear that the rugged beauty they were contemplating
was "the big breast." Shocking, perhaps, but there are
worse possibilities when lonely trappers are given freedom
to name landforms.

At any rate, the next step in the pioneering cycle, from
naming the peaks to climbing them, has been the object of
considerable debate. It seems that no less than three

Fault-block formation and glaciation are the principal forming powers
of the Tetons. (Photo by Don Owens)

parties have claimed the honor of the first ascent of the Grand Teton.

In 1872, the Hayden Survey, working under the auspices of the U.S. Geological Survey, was in the Teton Range, exploring and mapping the area. The members of this expedition were men who were accustomed to being in the mountains and often climbed high peaks to gain a vantage point from which to survey large areas of land and triangulate positions. Nonetheless, they were impressed by the Grand Teton and its neighbors, the Middle Teton and the South Teton. William Henry Jackson, the photographer for the expedition, made the first photographic plates of the Tetons, and the expedition leader, Capt. James Stevenson, and his lieutenant, Nathaniel Langford, decided to try to climb the highest of the Teton peaks, which they, knowing where their paychecks were coming from, had named Mount Hayden.

On July 28, Stevenson and Langford, accompanied by 12 of their men, left the main survey camp for the Grand. This first day was spent in reaching a high camp and surveying the Grand for route possibilities. The next day, armed with alpenstocks, ropes, and bacon sandwiches, they set out for the summit. En route, one man was disabled by rockfall, and eight others had called it quits by the time the party reached the Saddle, to the south of the Grand Teton. From the Saddle, Langford reported, the party climbed directly up the intervening snow, ice, and rock to the summit of the Grand. The party claimed the first ascent, but it found evidence of an earlier attempt in a small stone wall of unknown origins, called the Enclosure. Some claim that the wall was built by a trapper during an earlier attempt on the Grand, but it is generally believed to have been built by the Shoshone Indians in order to house braves when they climbed the mountains in quest of visions.

The Langford-Stevenson party took barometric readings on the summit, from which a summit elevation of 13,762 feet was computed. This is quite close to what was recognized for years as the elevation of the Grand (13,766), and it is even close to today's upgraded figure of 13,770 feet.

It would seem settled, then, that Langford and Stevenson climbed the Grand Teton first. Yet 26 years later, in 1898, a local man named William O. Owen, accompanied by the Rev. Frank Spalding and two other men, reached the summit of the Grand Teton and claimed the first ascent. This may have been due in part to frustration. Owen had been trying to climb the Grand for seven years before he succeeded, and naturally the thought that it might have been done in two days was mildly irritating. However, Owen also differed with the details Langford gave of his route (Stevenson was dead by this time), particularly with Langford's description of the portion above the Saddle.

Owen made a great deal of noise about all this, brushing aside the objective that gentlemen mountaineers ought to take one another's word on who made the first ascent. Owen pointed out that he had found no cairn on the summit, whereas he had not only left a cairn but had brought back photographic evidence of his ascent. After hearing all of Owen's impassioned rhetoric, the Wyoming legislature, more than 25 years later, recognized Owen as the first man to ascend the Grand Teton, an unsurprising action, since Owen had been a state employee for years. In 1929, when Grand Teton National Park was formed, a plaque was placed on the summit commemorating the Owen-Spalding ascent. Spalding's widow, Mrs. Emma Spalding, paid for the plaque.

Just to make matters more difficult, it appears that in 1893 an Army man named Kieffer reached the Grand Teton summit with two companions, but raised no commotion over the feat since he believed Langford and Stevenson had already made the climb. Officially the ascent is Owen's, but as mountaineers we must give serious attention to Landford's and Stevenson's claim.

Since the controversial first ascents, many routes have been put on the Grand Teton. Langford was the first of

Mount Owen and the Grand
Teton, from Hurricane Canyon.
(Photo by Don Owens)

many mountaineers to comment that the Grand Teton bore
a resemblance to the Matterhorn, and, like the Matterhorn, the Grand has a very steep side, the North Face.
This face has been the scene of several Grand Teton
classics. In 1936, Jack Durrance and Paul and Eldon
Petzoldt climbed most of the face, exiting to the north
ridge via a traverse ledge below the top. Thirteen years
later, Art Gilkey and Dick Pownall repeated the
Durrance-Petzoldt route, but were able to remain on the
face until just below the summit, where a traverse to the
north ridge was again taken. Then, in 1953, Richard
Emerson, Leigh Ortenberger, and Willi Unsoeld were able

to climb the North Face all the way to the top of the Grand. Years later, even this achievement was eclipsed when George and Greg Lowe, using newly invented super-gaiters for mixed snow and rock work, climbed the North Face in winter.

Today, the climber who wishes to climb the Grand must, as in all national parks, first register the climb with the Grand Teton National Park and get the park's permission to camp in the backcountry. This can be done at the Jenny Lake Ranger Station, located near the end of the one-way spur from Teton Park Road. Here, photograph files are kept of area routes and up-to-date information is always available. It is best to camp at Jenny Lake and to start for the high country as early the next day as possible, before sunrise if one does not wish to share the trail with a pack of others, all heading for the Grand.

The most popular route, and the one that is usually first taken up the Grand, is the *Owen-Spalding Route*. To do this route, one takes the trail into Garnet Canyon and then heads up to the Lower Saddle, an elevation gain of 4,900 feet for the day. From below, Tepee's Glacier is seen between the Exum Ridge and the East Ridge. The Lower Saddle is the stop for the night, after about eight hours of hiking. Early to bed is the best idea, as one should rise at around 3:00 A.M. to begin the climb to the summit.

Leaving the Lower Saddle, one climbs directly toward the Needle, a buttress at the higher end of the Lower Saddle. The Needle is passed on the left side, and trails are followed up a gully (actually an eroded basaltic dike) to the Upper Saddle. It is possible at this point to visit the Enclosure found by Langford and Stevenson, still here after all these years.

Next come the hardest fifth-class sections of the route, as the climb proceeds out on a ledge onto the West Face, past a boulder in the Belly Crawl, and then up chimneys and trails to the summit trail. The trail to the summit will be fairly distinct, and a register, a plaque, and a superb view await the climber on top.

The descent is done by downclimbing the *Owen-Spalding Route* or by making the two-rope rappel to the Upper Saddle. If all has gone well, a climber should be on the top before noon and well down the trail toward Jenny Lake by the time the afternoon thundershowers have started.

The Grand is also home to the most famous ice climb in America, the *Black Ice Couloir*, which has consistently good summer ice and also consistent summer stonefall. Jeff Lowe says that the *Black Ice Couloir* followed by the West Face is the best climb in the Tetons. He was in the first party to do this combination in the winter, when, he reports, the character of the *Black Ice Couloir* had changed somewhat:

> The ice in the Black Ice Couloir was so hard and brittle that screws could barely be placed, and the climbing therefore became far more committing than in the summer, particularly so since the points of your tools tended to do little more than grate on the surface of the ice.

However, Jeff points out that there are certain bonuses to climbing the Grand in winter. Though there may be avalanches, there is no rockfall (everything is frozen in place), and the mountain certainly isn't as crowded as it is during the peak summer months.

Winter climbing on the Grand is not recommended as an introduction to mountaineering. It requires a total rethinking of approaches, and entirely different equipment and techniques. Snowstorms of unexpected strength can pin a party down on the mountain for long periods, and members of the Lowe party carried both a snow shovel (that is, a stout aluminum scoop shovel, *not* the kind you use to clear the walk) and tents or bivouac sacks on their winter ascents to ensure themselves of shelter in such storms.

Mountaineers planning winter climbs in the Tetons must preregister at the Moose Visitor Center at the south end of the Grand Teton National Park, and should come prepared for temperatures well below zero at night.

The Grand Teton. (Photo by Don Owens)

There are at least two guides to climbing in the Teton Range, but the one which concentrates exclusively on this area is Leigh Ortenberger's *A Climber's Guide to the Teton Range*, which details routes on the Grand Teton and other peaks in the area of Grand Teton National Park. This book is recommended for anyone planning to climb in the Tetons, as it gives vital information about the area which should be known before one starts to climb. Equipped with this knowledge, and with the proper gear for the climb, a climber can more fully enjoy his journey into one of the most beautiful mountain ranges on earth. Mountaineers in need of further route assistance or of a guide for any climb, from the *Owen-Spalding* route to the *Black Ice Couloir*, should get in touch with Teton Mountaineering or the Exum School of Mountaineering, in Jackson Hole.

References

Atwood, Wallace W. *The Rocky Mountains*. New York: Vanguard Press, 1945. Pp. 281–82.

Bachman, B.B. II. "Underhill Ridge, Grand Teton." *Climbing*, July/August 1972, pp. 26–27.

Bueler, William M. *Mountains of the World*. Rutland, Vt.: Charles E. Tuttle Co., 1970. Pp. 34–38.

Bueler, William M. "Did They Climb the Grand?" *Off Belay*, no. 27 (June 1976), pp. 17–23.

Clark, Ronald W. *Men, Myths, and Mountains*. London: Weidenfeld and Nicolson, 1976. Pp. 37–38, 160, and 273.

Grand Teton National Park. "Winter Climbing Regulations for Grand Teton." *Off Belay*, no. 1 (January/February 1972), p. 46.

Grand Teton National Park. Information brochure.

Groves, Bruce. Interview. December 1977.

Jones, Chris. *Climbing in North America*. Berkeley: University of California Press for American Alpine Club, 1976. Pp. 30–31, 119–24, 309–14, and 376.

Lowe, Jeff. Letter of January 1978.

McMorrin, Ian, and Noyce, Wilfred. *World Atlas of Mountaineering*. London: Thomas Nelson and Sons, 1969. Pp. 168–69.

Matthews, William H. III. *A Guide to the National Parks: Their Landscape and Geology*. Garden City, N.Y.: Natural History Press, 1968. Vol. 1, pp. 166–78.

"Mount Rainier, Grand Teton Assaulted by the Masses." *Off Belay*, no. 1 (January/February 1972), p. 43.

"National Parks Mountaineering Traffic." *Off Belay*, no. 20 (April 1975), pp. 33–37.

Norton, Boyd. "The Grand Tetons." *Backpacker*, no. 12 (Winter 1975), pp. 25–30.

Tingey, Ralph. "How to Climb the Grand Teton." *Teton*, 1977, pp. 8–11+.

10

Mount Rainier

Fire and ice. The very combination of the words spins pictures of mystic incantations, of necromancers creating strange new worlds from nothingness. These are the elements of magic, and in the Middle Cascades of west-central Washington, there is a magic mountain made from fire and ice. The Northwest Coast Indians called it Tahoma, "The God Mountain," but today it is known as Mount Rainier.

The fire came aeons ago, in the form of primal flames from the depths of the earth. Mount Rainier is a volcano, a composite cone volcano which has been dormant, but not dead, for all of recorded history. The composite cone was formed because the volcano erupted in spasms, with periods of steady lava flow (of the type which generally forms shield volcanoes) between violent volcanic eruptions (of the type which generally form cinder cone volcanoes). Since two types of volcanic action were at work, the mountain combines the appearance of a shield volcano and a cinder cone volcano. Mount Rainier also has the look of a mountain which has had its top taken off, and this is a fairly

Now clad in ice and snow, the dormant volcano of Mount Rainier stands peacefully above Tipsoo Lake, near Chinook Pass. (Washington State Travel Photo)

accurate description of what took place. The mountain was once several hundred feet taller than it now is, but its thin-walled upper cone portion collapsed in on itself, fell down the mountain, or was blown away in an especially violent eruption.

After the volcanic fire came the ice. When the volcano had cooled and become dormant, snow began falling and collecting on the mountain's upper slopes in a process that still continues. Preserved by the cool temperatures of the upper mountain air, the snow settled in layers on the mountain. The layers compressed into ice, and as the masses of snow thus formed grew, they began to slide down the mountain, with the snow above continually feeding the tongues of ice below. Actually rivers of ice, these great, perpetually fed masses, called glaciers, acted as conveyors and excavators, picking up chunks of rock as they traveled downslope, grinding away at the ground they passed with this rock, and depositing the debris from this action in moraines at the bottom of the mountain.

This work was greatly accelerated during the Great Ice Age, when lower temperatures and heavy snowfall made the glaciers bigger, faster moving, and heavier. Thus, they were capable of moving more material from the mountain and of creating distinctive U-shaped glacial valleys on the flanks of Mount Rainier.

With the return of a warmer climate, many of the mountain's glaciers melted, leaving their valleys empty, and the remainder receded to smaller sizes, again becoming alpine glaciers (glaciers not made by climate alone). Yet, even when operating at today's reduced capacity, Mount Rainier has more active glaciation than does any

Mount Rainier is the most heavily glaciated mountain in the contiguous 48 states. (Courtesy National Park Service)

other mountain in the lower 48 states. For those who love
to climb snow and ice, it is truly a mecca.

The discovery of Mount Rainier is credited to Capt.
George Vancouver of the English Royal Navy, in the
1790s, who named the great snow-clad peak in honor of
the soon-to-be Rear Adm. Peter Rainier, a friend. Vancouver was not, however, an explorer of Mount Rainier, as
the closest he ever got to it was the deck of his ship, about
40 miles away in Puget Sound.

The Northwest Coast Indians had made some prelimi-
nary attempts to reach the top of Rainier, but its height
and their religious awe prevented them from ever getting
beyond the lower glaciers. The curiosity-generated urge to
stand on top of the great peak was strong, but the force of
tradition and myth was even stronger—it was believed
that any man who reached the summit of Tahoma would
not be allowed to return to his people alive.

The white settlers in the Northwest had no such mythi-
cal tradition, however, and though they had great awe for
the mountain, in their case it was the curiosity that won
out.

There are reports that survey parties may have made
their way to the summit of Mount Rainier as early as
1855, but none of these stories has been confirmed by
summit evidence of written records, and it is doubtful that
a survey team would have made the ascent without making a careful record of the climb. In 1857, some Army men
attempted the climb, and they managed to reach the upper
part of the Kautz Glacier before turning back. It was not
until August 1870, however, that a party made the ascent
and publicly reported having reached the highest point on
the mountain, 14,410-foot Columbia Crest, at the junction
of the volcano's twin craters.

This ascent was made by Philemon Beecher Van Trump
and General Hazard Stevens, two adventurous young men
who made up their minds to climb the peak with the
experienced mountaineer Edward Coleman. The three got
together horses, supplies, and a brass plaque with their

names on it for the summit, and then set out from Olympia after a grand send-off from their neighbors. Coleman did not last too long. He was accustomed to the more civilized travel and climbing in the Alps, and his companions soon left him behind, probably with the suggestion that he should go back to the Alps.

Van Trump and Stevens made their way from Olympia to the vicinity of Rainier, where they employed a Klickitat Indian named Sluiskin as a guide to take them as far as timberline. Sluiskin would have made a good commercial guide, as he charged his clients by the day and took them to the mountain by a much longer route than necessity demanded.

At length, however, the south side of the mountain was gained, and Van Trump and Stevens, after telling Sluiskin to break camp and tell their friends that they had died if they did not return in three days, set off for the top. They followed Gibraltar Rock, on a route later known as the *Gib Route*, and reached Point Success (14,150 feet) that evening. Seeing that the actual summit was still 260 feet above them and to the north of them, they became the first of many mountaineers to bed down for the night in the steam-jet cavities of the crater and to find that doing so steams only one side of the body while the other becomes frosted. The following morning, slightly damp and cranky, Van Trump and Stevens arose to try for the summit. The weather, however, was turning. A cloud cap was closing in on the summit, and thinking this to be a full-fledged storm cloud, the pair began to consider descent. The whiteout, or near whiteout, made even descent difficult, however, so Van Trump and Stevens went to the true summit (Columbia Crest), left their plaque (with Coleman's name scratched out), and then, convinced that the weather was not improving, made their way through the thickening mist to Gibraltar Rock for the descent.

On the way down, Van Trump slipped and gashed his leg, but the two made camp safely, Van Trump's leg was bandaged, and after a dinner of pancakes, Van Trump and

Stevens settled back to enjoy the fire. At this point, Sluiskin returned to camp, having been gone to tend the horses, and only after great persuasion could he be convinced that the two climbers were not specters of his clients, killed by the gods at the top of Tahoma. Once Sluiskin realized that Van Trump and Stevens were indeed alive, he offered his hearty congratulations to the first climbers of Mount Rainier.

Mount Rainier was established as a national park in 1899, and it has had a very active mountaineering history ever since. For years, the *Gib Route* was widely used by clubs and guided parties to reach the top, but when rockfall destroyed part of the route, this climb was largely abandoned. The pace of Mount Rainier climbing was accelerated quite a bit as the 20th century advanced. In 1935, Wolf Bauer and Jack Hossack tackled Ptarmigan Ridge successfully in a two-day climb, and soon thereafter

Mount Adams (left) and Mount Saint Helens, both more than forty air miles away, can be seen easily in this view, looking south from the summit of Mount Rainier. (Courtesy National Park Service)

Liberty Ridge was also climbed. These routes, both on the more difficult North Face of Mount Rainier, were quite a jump from the *Gib Route*. In 1936, Delmar Fadden made an unauthorized winter solo attempt on Rainier. He was killed by a fall and exposure, but a roll of film in his pocket contained pictures of the summit.

Another illegal solo climb made Rainier history in 1961, when Charles Bell made the first ascent of the steep true North Face of the mountain, the Willis Wall. Bell's story was challenged by other climbers, so he returned in 1962 to resolo it with a camera and prove his claim. The Willis Wall still holds a reputation as one of the hardest routes on Mount Rainier. In 1970, however, Jim Wickwire and Alex Bertulis did this hard climb the hard way, making their ascent in winter.

For those who want something adventurous to do after arriving at the top of Mount Rainier, there is always caving. The same year that the Willis Wall was climbed in winter, Lou Whittaker and Lee Nelson made underground (or underice) crossings of the summit craters, in melted passageways beneath the summit ice. Since then, numerous melted passageways have been mapped in this bizarre environment at the top of Washington's tallest mountain. Other strange activities on Rainier include an orbit of the peak at about the 10,000-foot level in 1968, and the usual odd ascents associated with a popular mountain—the young, the old, the nude . . .

Contemporary climbers who wish to mountaineer on Tahoma at any point above the 7,000-foot level must register their intentions with a climbing ranger and sign in on completion of their climb. Solo climbing, formerly prohibited, is now allowed if a climber has the permission of the park superintendant.

The authorities at Mount Rainier wish to make it clear to climbers that Mount Rainier is a high and glaciated mountain, with all the hazards of any such mountain. It was used as a training ground for mountaineering troops in World War II and for the members of the 1963 American Everest Expedition. It is no place for the casual or the ill-equipped, and 36 serious accidents in the five years from 1972 to 1977 have been the results of poor preparation.

It is pointed out by climbing rangers that good physical conditioning is important for a successful Rainier climb, and parties of three or more in summer and four or more in winter are recommended for safety. The national park officials have a recommended equipment list which includes crampons, lugged boots, hard hats, carabiners, climbing rope, sleeping bags, mittens, Prusik slings, ice axes, a first-aid kit, glacier cream, food, flashlights, maps and compasses, pitons, ice screws, pulleys, a stove and fuel, trail wands, a tent or a bivvy sack, and wool, down, and

Mount Rainier, from Stevens Canyon Road. (Washington State Travel Photo)

waterproof clothing. This is for a group attempting an average climb in summer. The park officials recommend that in winter, heavy sleeping bags, down pants and mitts, snowshoes or skis, expedition tents, a sturdy snow shovel, at least 200 trail wands, extra food and fuel, a two-way radio, an altimeter, avalanche cords, and additional rope also be carried.

Rainier is generally a multiday climb, and in addition to the climbing permit, permission to camp on the mountain must be obtained. For the usual route to the top, from Paradise, one camps at Camp Muir, which has a capacity of 100 persons, and then one follows the Ingraham Glacier to Columbia Crest.

For those who desire such services, Rainier Mountaineering, in Tacoma, offers climbing instruction, seminars, and guided climbs to the summit, and for those not used to glacier crossing and alpine mountaineering, such services are well worth considering. Rainier Mountaineering, run by internationally acclaimed climber Lou Whittaker is, without a doubt, one of the most outstanding guide services in North America.

Mount Rainier offers extensive snow and glacier climbing in an area that is easy to reach and somewhat less hostile than other peaks of equal snow cover. Those planning expeditions to high altitudes or the Arctic will find that Rainier, particularly in winter, provides a good shakedown climb. And those not bound for faraway places will find that the slopes of Tahoma offer various degrees of difficulty, almost any challenge a climber might wish to face. A recommended guide is Fred Beckey's *Cascade Alpine Guide*, and *The Challenge of Rainier*, by Dee Molenaar, is recommended general reading.

References

Abraght, Nona. Interview. December 1977.

Bishop, Barry C. "Mount Rainier: Testing Ground for Mount Everest." *National Geographic*, May 1963, pp. 688–711.

Foss, Hal. "Orbit of Mount Rainier." *Summit*, May 1969, pp. 23–26.

Jones, Chris. *Climbing in North America*. Berkeley: University of California Press for American Alpine Club, 1976. Pp. 143, 145–47, 303–36, and 376.

Martin, Dick. "More on the Mount Rainier Controversy." *Off Belay*, no. 26 (April 1976), pp. 31–35.

Molenaar, Dee. "Solo Winter Ascent of Rainier." *Summit*, July/August 1971, pp. 19–23.

Molenaar, Dee. "Rainier: The Mountain That Is God." *Backpacker*, no. 6 (Summer 1974), pp. 32–36+.

Mount Rainier National Park. "Climbing Mount Rainier" (regulations brochure).

Nelson, Lee. "Spelunking on Mount Rainier." *Summit*, April 1971, p. 3.

Nelson, Lee. "Mount Rainier—Willis Wall." *Summit*, May 1972, pp. 7–8.

Penberthy, Larry. "On the Mount Rainier Controversy." *Off Belay*, no. 24 (December 1975), pp. 17–18.

Spezia, John. "Winter Traverse of Mount Rainier." *Summit*, May 1973, pp. 3–7.

Van Trump, Philemon Beecher. "Mount Rainier: Its First Ascent—1870." *Off Belay*, no. 17 (October 1974), pp. 20–25+.

11

Mount Whitney

Mount Whitney has all the grace and grandeur of the deposed monarch that it is. At 14,495 feet, Whitney was once the tallest mountain in the United States. It lost that title, not because it shrank, but because the statehood of Alaska ushered into power a number of taller peaks, led by Denali at 20,320 feet. When Alaska became a state, Mount Whitney was reduced from a monarch to a princeling—the tallest mountain in the 48 contiguous states.

Whitney was not discovered until July 1864, when two members of the California State Geological Survey, Clarence King and Dick Cotter, sighted the peak from the summit of a neighboring mountain. Its height surprised them. The Survey had already assumed Mount Shasta to be the highest American peak, but this new summit appeared to be even higher. It was named in honor of Josiah Whitney, founder and director of the California Geological Survey. In accordance with the custom of the day, the summit was declared inaccessible on the basis of height, and King returned to his camp to report his find.

The first view of Mount Whitney that most visitors get is this one, from Whitney Portal in Inyo National Forest. (Courtesy U.S. Forest Service)

King returned in 1867 to try to climb the peak, but he confused his bearings and climbed the wrong peak, a point which was later stressed by a former Survey member, who reported having ridden his mule to the summit that King had climbed.

King finally made it to the top of the real Mount Whitney in 1873, but at least two parties had beaten him to the top. The group generally recognized as the first ascenders consisted of a group of local men on a fishing trip, who demanded that the mountain be renamed Fisherman's Peak in their honor. A bill to this effect was introduced into the California state legislature and was vetoed by the governor.

The steep East Face of Whitney is the rock climbers' face. To the left is Keeler Needle. (Photo by Rocky Rockwell)

A long escarpment forms the Whitney massif, from Mount Muir (left), through the Pinnacles, to Mount Whitney. (Photo by Rocky Rockwell)

A High Sierra landscape. Mount Whitney is to the left, and Mount Carillon is to the right. (Photo by Rocky Rockwell)

Today, most people get to the summit of Mount Whitney via the Forest Service's Mount Whitney Trail. The head of this relatively easy trail can be reached by taking the Mount Whitney Road turnoff, from Highway 6–395, at Lone Pine and following Mount Whitney Road to Whitney Portal. The trail begins at Whitney Portal, 13 miles from Lone Pine.

The National Park Service suggests that trips to Mount Whitney begin from Whitney Portal early in the afternoon, and that an overnight camp be made at Outpost Camp or Trail Camp. Outpost Camp is 3½ miles from Whitney Portal, and Trail Camp is 6 miles from Whitney Portal.

The next morning's start should be early, probably before dawn if one is camped at Outpost Camp. A little more than eight miles from Whitney Portal, just past Trail Crest, the Mount Whitney Trail intersects with the John Muir Trail near a peak called Mount Muir. From the intersection it is less than two miles to the summit of Mount Whitney and the return to Whitney Portal is usually made the same day.

Since Mount Whitney is a popular peak, it has been necessary to impose a number of regulations on the use of the trail. To begin with, only 75 people per day are allowed to leave Whitney Portal for the summit. Those who wish to make sure that they will get to make the trip would be well advised to reserve a quota reservation, or wilderness permit, by writing to the Mount Whitney Ranger Station, Inyo National Forest, P.O. Box 8, Lone Pine, California 93545, and stating how many people in the party would like to go from Whitney Portal to Mount Whitney on which dates. This should be done anytime after February 1 of the year in which a trip is planned— the earlier the better. The Forest Service will send either a no-vacancy notice or a confirmation of the reservation, with instructions telling where the reservation should be picked up. It is important to note that reservations are held only until noon of the date desired and are then given away on a first-come, first-served basis. So, even if one is

The summits of Mount Whitney and Keeler Needle are very unsummitlike in this photo—they are the two flat spots to the left. (Photo by Rocky Rockwell)

The surprising West Slope of Mount Whitney. (Photo by Rocky Rockwell)

not leaving for the first camp until the afternoon, the permit must be picked up in the morning.

It is also important to note that, since Mount Whitney and the surrounding areas are designated wilderness, the "camps" are not camps *per se*. They have no toilet facilities, fireplaces, picnic tables, and so on. Campsite restrictions include camping on soil only, camping well away from trails and water supplies, and using "cat holes" as toilets. No soap can be allowed to enter any body of water; all garbage (including cigarette butts) must be carried out; and only gas stoves can be used for cooking, since

Mount Whitney is the high point on a long ridge, to the right of center.
(Courtesy U.S. Forest Service)

there is no firewood for camp use, and it is illegal to build
fire rings anyhow. In general, the backpacking ethic of
leaving a campsite in better condition than one found it
should be followed to the hilt. Ideally, the only sign that
one has been at a campsite should be a lack of dew on the
ground where the tent stood.

Although the Mount Whitney Trail is a truly enjoyable
way to get to the top of Whitney, it is at best a class 2
ascent, and perhaps not even that, since the rough parts of
the trail were blasted clear after World War II. Those who
wish to do some climbing to gain the summit should leave
the Mount Whitney Trail a half-mile from Whitney Portal
and get on the North Fork Trail instead. A camp is
generally made at Clyde Meadows or Eastface Lake, and a
short hike from either of these will bring one to the bottom
of the East Face of Mount Whitney—the climber's side.

Mount Whitney, from the northwest. (Photo by Bill Jones, courtesy National Park Service)

The *Mountaineer's Route* is the easiest way up the East Face, a class 3 ascent up a large couloir between the East Buttress and the North Arete, but it is worth doing simply because by climbing it one follows in the footsteps of John Muir, the great Sierra pioneer. The East Buttress is a bit more challenging, with at least one fifth-class pitch. The *East Face Route* has two fifth-class pitches, and it can be varied to suit the tastes and expertise of the climber. If the East Face is expanded to include the entire area of the eastern Whitney escarpment, routes of nearly every level of difficulty can be found, including the nearby Keeler Needle, only recently freed at 5.10. Getting down from the East Face is usually done by taking the Muir and Whitney trails back to Whitney Portal (provided that one has traveled light enough to carry everything up the face, thus avoiding a long detour to pick up the tent, etc.).

As is usual in a government preserve, climbers should check with the authorities before setting out, in order to get approval on campsites and intended routes. The

An aerial view of the East Face of Mount Whitney. (Photo by Bill Jones, courtesy National Park Service)

rangers generally recommend taking hard hats, and they are right. The East Face has some natural rockfall, augmented by people who accidentally kick stones loose as they walk to the summit on the trail above. A time schedule should be given to the rangers and stuck to, and climbers should sign out before leaving Whitney Portal, to spare the rangers the nuisance and expense of an unnecessary search-and-rescue trip into the backcountry.

Mountaineer's Guide to the High Sierra, by Andrew Smatko and Hervey Voge, covers the Mount Whitney area and the bulk of the Sierra Nevada. Also quite useful is Walt Wheelock and Tom Condon's *Climbing Mount Whitney*, which, though more dated than the *Mountaineer's Guide*, is considerably more detailed in regard to Mount Whitney and highly enjoyable to read.

Mount Whitney is enjoyable, whether it is climbed by trail or by technical route. It is also a textbook example of alpine climatic changes, as one goes from the desert at Lone Pine to the arctic zone at the summit. The trip to the top is educational and memorable, and the fact that the mountain is no longer America's highest has not changed this one bit.

References

Bueler, William M. *Mountains of the World*. Rutland, Vt.: Charles E. Tuttle Co., 1970. Pp. 51–55.

Crausaz, Winston. "Four Views of Mount Whitney." *Summit*, August 1976, pp. 27–30.

Jones, Chris. *Climbing in North America*. Berkeley: University of California Press for American Alpine Club, 1976. Pp. 21–25, 127–29.

Matthews, William H. III. *A Guide to the National Parks*. Garden City, N.Y.: Natural History Press, 1968. Vol 1, pp. 326, 341, and 342.

Rowell, Galen. "The Needle Goes Free." *Mariah*, Summer 1977, pp. 26–32.

Smatko, Andrew J., and Voge, Hervey H. *Mountaineer's Guide to the High Sierra*. San Francisco: Sierra Club, 1972. Pp. 307–8.

Wheelock, Walt, and Condon, Tom. *Climbing Mount Whitney*. Glendale, Calif.: La Siesta Press, 1960.

Part 3
Big Rocks

The European climbing tradition taught American climbers how to rock-climb and mountaineer. Snow and ice technique, extended alpine rock climbing, and mixed snow-and-rock climbing were all common practice in Europe before American climbers entered these fields.

But American climbers were fast learners. This adaptiveness, coupled with the American knack for technology, was to quickly prepare the mountaineers of the United States for new horizons. It was in the field of big rock climbing that Americans took their first steps into new fields.

Big rocks lie somewhere in the penumbra of mountaineering classification. Too large to be crags, too small to be mountains, and devoid of the nonextreme borders and the flat width of the big wall, big rocks can be described as big crags with small big wall routes on all sides. Although not unique to the United States, big rocks happened to catch the fancy of American climbers as the sport of climbing was just coming to maturity in this country, and it is on these monoliths that American climbing showed its first great signs of originality, both in character and area.

The big rocks stand as mileposts of progress in U.S. climbing. Once climbed, they marked the way to the ascent of the even larger big walls and to a whole new area of climbing endeavor in the stone towers which rise from the prairies and deserts surrounding the Rocky Mountains. Big in themselves, these rocks were the key to even bigger things, and the ascents of these rocks were the warning rumbles of an American climbing spirit to be reckoned with.

12

Devils Tower

In Crook County, Wyoming, within sight of the Little Missouri Buttes and rising to a height of 5,117 feet above sea level and of 1,280 feet above the nearby Belle Fourche River, is a geologic oddity unlike any other rock formation in North America. From a distance, the rock formation has been favorably compared to a gargantuan petrified tree stump. Close at hand, it is shown to be composed of great six-sided columns of igneous rock, some of which have toppled to the base of the great shaft. The effect is that of the great stone temple of a long-dead race of giants.

To the Sioux and the Crow, this stone tower has been a shrine, a rallying point, and a mystical landmark. They believed that the tower had been formed by magic, when a group of youths were being pursued by bears. The youths entreated the Great Spirit to save them, and the Great Spirit caused the low boulder on which they stood to grow high into the air. The bears clawed at the rock as it grew, leaving long scars which remain to this day, but they could not reach their quarry. In commemoration of this

Devils Tower, from the southeast. (Photo by Rick Tapia)

event, the rock was named Mateo Tepee, "The Grizzly Bears Ledge."

Another legend said that the bad gods used the formation as a drum during rainstorms, and in this legend Mateo Tepee was referred to as the Bad Gods Tower. The legend was related to Col. Richard I. Dodge as he explored the area in 1875. Dodge translated the name to its Christian equivalent, and the landmark appeared on maps of the region as the Devil's Tower.

Colonel Dodge's discovery was of immense interest to geologists of the era, and conjecture concerning the origins of the Tower began immediately. (The Indian legend, however likable, was not plausible.) A theory which won widespread support was that the Tower was a core remnant of a great volcano whose exterior slopes had eroded. This theory was popular for a number of years, but geomorphologists now question it. They point out that the regular shapes of the columns are the results of crystallization of a type which would not have taken place in a volcano. It is now generally believed that the Tower is an ancient igneous intrusion, a dome-shaped mass of rock which had pushed its way in liquid form up through the earth but had not succeeded in breaking the surface. The dome slowly cooled, and the ages wore the soft layers of the surrounding rock away, leaving the harder phonolite porphyry exposed to the air. Both theories involved incredible amounts of erosion, a generally slow process. The tower, then, would have to be quite old, a conclusion which is supported by the findings of Dr. William Bassett, of Brookhaven National Laboratory. Using potassium-argon dating techniques, Dr. Bassett has come to the conclusion that Devils Tower is more than 40 million years old.

Geologists, explorers, and early settlers of northeastern Wyoming admired Devils Tower for a variety of reasons, but they did not expect the Tower to be climbed. The ominous appearance of the rock, the steepness of its sides, and the smoothness of its surface combined to support the belief that Mateo Tepee's summit was unattainable. That belief was soon shattered.

In 1893, the Crook County Independence Day committee was wrestling with that immortal enemy of holiday planners, public apathy. The committee wanted desperately to make the annual Fourth of July picnic a success, but none of the usual events of the times, the roping contests or the riding competitions, seemed capable of drawing the desired crowd. The problem was one to make men dry. A bottle was passed, and once deep into it, Will Rogers (not *the* Will Rogers), a local rancher, came up with a unique solution to the problem. Rogers announced that he would climb Devils Tower on the Fourth of July. This announcement was greeted with wagers, and plans were made to publicize the historic undertaking.

Will had placed himself in an awkward position. At

Devils Tower, from the northwest. (Courtesy National Park Service)

stake were his honor, his fortune, and the success of the picnic, not to mention his life. Will studied the Tower, and Will formed a plan.

On reconnaissance trips to the Tower, Rogers and his neighbor, Willard Ripley, found bad news and good. The bad news was that the Tower was surrounded by smooth and perpendicular columns. The good news was that the columns were shorter in some places than in others. By following a broken, sloping shoulder on the south side of the Tower, the pair were able to reach two columns which started well up on the rock and ended in a ledge about one-third of the way from the top. The ledge looked large, and the way above appeared easy, but the problem of surmounting the pillars to reach the ledge remained. Will knew he had solved the problem when he noticed that a constant gap of three-to-four inches ran between the columns all the way to the ledge.

With Ripley's help, Rogers began cutting what appeared to be fence posts from nearby trees. The posts were carried to the base of the columns, and when a goodly supply had been assembled, Will produced a mallet and began pounding the posts into the crack between the columns. By standing on the post he had just driven. Will was able to inch his way up the Tower, making a ladder as he went. Two-by-fours were added to the outsides of the posts as bracing, and within six weeks Rogers and Ripley had a ladder to the large ledge, now known as "the Meadows." The way above proved as easy as it had looked; an unofficial ascent was made to place a flagpole, and the stage was set.

On July 4, 1893, in an event billed as "better than the World's Fair," in a costume provided by the ladies of Deadwood, South Dakota, and bearing a flag supplied by the ladies of Spearfish, South Dakota, Will Rogers stepped to the base of his ladder. The band played martial music, and minutes later Rogers appeared at the top of Devils Tower and flung Old Glory to the breeze. Rogers' name had been saved and his wagers won, and when the flag soon fell to the picnic grounds, he increased his fortune further by cutting up the banner and selling the bits to the crowd. Indeed, Rogers' reputation seemed clinched, when, from the top of Devils Tower, there came the sound of young voices. A group of small boys had climbed Will's ladder. The crowd roared, the parents of the young adventurers scolded, and the boys came down, bringing with them the tarnished remains of Will Rogers' short-lived glory.

Rogers' fence-post ladder remained the only viable route up Devils Tower for the more than 20 people who climbed it between 1893 and 1927, when the ladder was closed to use. With it, Will had proved the experts wrong, and they quickly corrected their statement, claiming that the Tower would never be scaled by conventional mountaineering methods. This, too, would be proved wrong.

In 1936, while returning from a second ascent of the North Ridge of the Grand Teton, Fritz Weissner talked his companions into making a side trip to the "unclimbable tower" he had heard about. The columned giant appealed to Weisner's crack-climbing instincts, and he immediately resolved to climb it. More than mere resolve would be

From this view of the
Southwest Face, it is easy to
see why early visitors thought
the Tower unclimbable.
(Photo by Bruce Groves)

necessary, however. In 1906, President Teddy Roosevelt
had declared Devils Tower the first national monument,
so, as is true on any National Park Service property,
permission was required to make the climb. Weissner
applied for permission, the National Park Service refused
to grant it, and intervention on the part of the Alpine Club
was necessary to convince the authorities that Weissner
was dedicated, not suicidal.

Weissner returned the following year, accompanied by
Bill House and Lawrence Coveney. A line was decided on
near the Shoulder, a prowlike projection on the south side
of the Tower. The first attempt was beaten back by a
particularly obstinate bush near the bottom of the Tower,
but gymnastics overcame the vegetation on the following
day, and the party made their way up cracks and stem

chimneys to establish *Weissner* (5.7), the first climber's route up Devils Tower. It is a fair indication of the party's skill that the climb took less than five hours, a respectable time for a three-man party on that route, especially on a first ascent.

In 1938, Jack Durrance and Harry Butterworth made the second ascent of Devils Tower via the *Durrance Route* (5.6), a jam crack and squeeze chimney route which, despite its fairly advanced rating, remains the easiest route on the Tower. Having been climbed by one unorthodox route and two climbers' lines, the Tower might have been expected to withdraw itself from public attention, but that was not to happen. There was a parachutist named Charles Hopkins, and Charley had made a bet . . .

Actually, Charley had made more than a bet. Partly to publicize himself as a stunt parachutist, partly to save face, and partly to win a $50 wager, Hopkins parachuted from a passing airplane to the top of Devils Tower. That part went fine. The trouble began when Hopkins discovered that the 1,000-foot abseil rope that the plane had dropped to him for his descent from the summit was tangled beyond use. After several attempts to unsnarl the rope, Hopkins gave up and began cutting the line into 100-foot lengths, but cold and wet weather soon froze even these into useless, tangled hunks. Much to the nation's amazement, the Park Service's ire, and Hopkins' embarrassment, he discovered that he could not get down from the Tower.

The situation was, to say the least, awkward.

To begin with, Hopkins had made his jump in October, never a month famous for balmy weather in Wyoming. Concern was expressed for his survival, and a series of airdrops provided him with an Army tent, a sleeping bag, a portable stove, coal, firewood, blankets, hot-water bottles, and sufficient rations for a small regiment. This was in 1941, and the National Monument staff (which had not been forewarned of the jump anyway) had no one capable of climbing the monolith, so a request for two climbing

Fluted columns form Devils Tower. To the Indians, the cracks suggested claw marks. To early settlers, they looked like tree bark. To a climber, they are routes. (Courtesy National Park Service)

rangers was sent to Rocky Mountain National Park. The rangers arrived, but Devils Tower was quite beyond their usual scope of climbing, and they had to adjust as they climbed—very slowly.

By Saturday, October 4, Hopkins had spent three days atop the Tower, and the situation was beginning to have all the earmarks of a disaster. The climbing rangers were actively seeking the assistance of a person who had climbed the Tower; investigations were being made as to the feasibility of landing a skiplane on the summit; the Sikorsky Aircraft Company was being petitioned for the use of one of its newly invented helicopters; and the Goodyear blimp, *Reliance*, was setting out from Akron, Ohio, in the hope of hoisting Hopkins from the rock. Hopkins, meanwhile, was dividing his time between consoling himself with snacks from his pile of supplies and peering down forlornly upon the ever-growing crowd of spectators.

When bad weather detained the Goodyear blimp at Fort
Wayne, Indiana, and help seemed beyond reach, a surplus
of help appeared. Rock climbers all over the nation realized that names were to be made at Devils Tower, and
volunteers were suddenly everywhere. Jack Durrance and
Paul Petzoldt, rivals for the same mountain-guiding fran-
chise, both hastened to the Tower, demanding to be the
saviors of Charles Hopkins. National Park Service officials, understandably upset at being in the center of the
awkward predicament, were unprepared to judge who
should rescue him and finally decided to send everybody.
Durrance led the rescue, but no fewer than seven beaming
hopefuls were hard on his heels, ready to take the lead if
he should falter. Hopkins was brought down (Petzoldt was
accused of hogging the press coverage of the rescue), and
the wayward parachutist had the cheek to tell reporters
that he had gained five pounds while waiting to be
rescued. He had spent almost a week marooned on the
summit of Devils Tower. H. P. Joyner, the national monument superintendent, summed up the official viewpoint
this way, "My first consideration will be for Mr. Hopkins'
comfort. My second will be to prevent any repetition of
this sort of thing."

The Tower's penchant for publicity still surfaces from
time to time. In 1956, to celebrate the national monument's
50th anniversary, a climber's week was held, with more
than 200 climbers, climbing, partying, and giving rescue
demonstrations. In 1977, Devils Tower was depicted as the
focal point of a flying saucer invasion in Columbia Pictures' *Close Encounters of the Third Kind,* a science fiction
blockbuster that placed Devils Tower alongside the Eiger
and the Matterhorn on the exclusive list of mountains
which have played name roles in major motion pictures.

For climbers, however, the Tower's exceptionally sound
rock, unique columnar structure, and reputation for fine
climbing remain the major points of attraction. Aid routes,
such as the *McCarthy West Face* route (5.8, A3) and Royal
Robbins' aptly named *Window* (IV, 5.6, A4), abound for

The Leaning Column, easily identifiable in the center of the photo, forms the first pitch of the *Durrance Route*, the standard route on Devils Tower. (Photo by Don Owens)

the aid climber or the free climbing expert seeking new horizons. Old and new free routes, such as *Soler* (5.9) and another Robbins creation, *Danse Macabre* (5.10+), continue to offer fine challenges to the climber visiting the area, and the area's popularity is reflected in the list of more than 5,000 climbers who have entered their names in the register on the broad, prairielike summit of this unique rock.

Climbers no longer have to apply for permission to climb Devils Tower, although preclimb registration remains mandatory. Helmets are strongly encouraged, and the *Durrance Route*, once a mandatory first climb for Tower climbers, is still the route that the National Park Service suggests starting with. Even those who climb well above the 5.6 level would be wise to do the *Durrance* first. It gets climbers acquainted with the surface and structure of the rock, and introduces them to the ofttimes spectacular sequences of moves required in Devils Tower climbing.

The Meadows rappel from Devils Tower. (Photo by Don Owens)

The *Durrance Route*, for example, consists of face-, then jam-, then stem-climbing a first pitch up a leaning column to the right of the Shoulder. The next pitch is a sustained combination body jam and wide stem between two columns which flare apart at the top, where an awkward reversal of position (the crux) puts one in position to reach to the right and mantle to a belay. Next comes the aptly named Cussin' Crack, a squeeze chimney leading to a sparsely protected around-the-corner traverse. A flake, another crack, and an overhanging chockstone bring one to a six-foot leap from ledge to ledge, after which the summit is just a short scramble away through the rattlesnake-infested Meadows. Tower descent is by rappel from permanently placed double eyebolts.

A Climber's Guide to Devils Tower National Monument, by Curt Haire and Terry Rypkema, was brought out in late 1977, and can be purchased in the area, or climbers can ask to see the route descriptions and photos kept on file in the national monument Visitors' Center. Camping is available at the national monument for a nominal fee, and showers, food, and a launderette are available just outside the monument boundaries. An early start is a good idea for all climbs, as this can eliminate the necessity of climbing in the noonday sun and the prospect of having to pose for, or appear impolite to, the hordes of camera-toting tourists.

References

Bassett, William A. "Potassium-Argon Age of Devils Tower, Wyoming." *Science*, 27 October 1961, p. 1373.

Bird, Dick. "Devils Tower, Durrance Route." *Climbing*, no. 6 (March/April 1971), pp. 18–20.

Clark, Ronald W. *Men, Myths, and Mountains*. London: Weidenfeld and Nicolson, 1976. Pp. 131–32, 159–60.

Anonymous. "Devils Tower 1893." *Off Belay*, no. 1 (January/February 1972), pp. 7–9.

Haire, Curt, and Rypkema, Terry. *A Climber's Guide to Devils Tower National Monument*. Devils Tower, Wyo.: Terry Rypkema and Curt Haire, 1977.

Heald, Weldon F. "Lodge of the Grizzly Bear." *National Parks*, December 1962, pp. 8–10.

INS wirephoto stories concerning Hopkins' rescue, 3–7, October 1941.

Jones, Chris. *Climbing in North America*. Berkeley: University of California Press for American Alpine Club, 1976. Pp. 169–70.

13

Shiprock

In the desert west of Farmington, New Mexico, only a few miles from the Colorado and Arizona state lines, a plug of volcanic rhyolite rises 1,700 feet from the flatlands of the Navaho Indian Reservation to an altitude of 7,178 feet. The Navaho call it Tsae-bid-tae, "The Great Stone Bird," and view the rock and the area surrounding it with an easily appreciated deep spiritual respect. Early travelers in the area saw the landmark from a distance and likened the summit towers—the wings of the Great Stone Bird—to a schooner's sails. The simile seemed so appropriate that the plug became known as Shiprock.

Religious shrine, landmark, scenic attraction—Shiprock served many purposes in the New Mexico countryside, but it was not until the 1930s that anyone seriously entertained the idea of climbing it. Steep sides, loose rock, and an almost enchanted aura held early climbers in awe of Shiprock, but in 1939, after the successful ascents of such improbable Western climbs as Lizard Head and Devils Tower, Shiprock seemed a problem whose time had come.

Many of the choice routes in the area surrounding the

Rockies had been plucked off by outsiders—visiting East Coast climbers or members of Southern California's Sierra Club. Fritz Weissner's success on Devils Tower seemed a particularly bitter pill to swallow for the accomplished rock climbers in Wyoming and Colorado, who had let the prize of the first ascent be snatched from under their very noses. Colorado climbers Bob Ormes and Mel Griffith were determined to keep Shiprock from being stolen as well, and after closely inspecting the rock in 1936, they organized a four-man assault for 1937.

The Colorado climbers trained under the famed Rocky Mountain climber Albert Ellingwood and honed their skills in the Garden of the Gods. They waited until the cool month of October for their desert effort, scouted the rock and found a seemingly plausible route on the west side, and armed themselves for the attack with soft-iron pitons

Shiprock, East Face. (Photo by Gary Garbert, courtesy Bill Forrest)

and rubber-soled sneakers, the best rock-climbing footwear available. From earlier trips, they were able to work out a climbable line to a finger of basalt which seemed to offer a key to the summit above.

But high above the Navaho grazing lands, the going was getting quite tough. Two-man stands were employed to place pitons, and the crumbling rock offered few cracks that would hold a pin well. Ormes took the lead, going several feet above his last protection and hanging from slowly disintegrating holds as he searched for a place to nail a pin. No cracks presented themselves, and just as Ormes was ready to back off, the footholds below him give way and he was hurtling headfirst toward the sands below.

This was in 1937. Nylon rope was not then known to mountaineers, and the hard-steel piton was still years away. Even worse, belay methods were at best casual, and the fall of a leader was generally fatal. Luckily for Ormes, his belayer, Bill House, had a death grip on the rope. House was jerked up and off his perch, but he refused to let go, and Ormes was miraculously saved after a 30-foot fall. Another try was made, and the piton which had held Ormes was extracted. It was bent almost double and had started to break. This was enough for the climbers. They packed their gear and left the Great Stone Bird in peace.

That peace was soon to be broken. Only two years after the Colorado group had given up Shiprock as unclimbable, it was visited by the feared outsiders—the Rock Climbing Section of the Sierra Club.

The members of the RCS had several points in their favor. They had climbed extensively in California, including long routes in the famed Yosemite Valley. Mel Griffith, in a very generous gesture, made a six-hour drive from Colorado to Shiprock, to share firsthand his route information from the first attempt and to wish the Californians luck. The RCS also had two secret weapons. The first was the dynamic belay, a method of catching a falling leader with a controlled feed-out of the rope, which had been practiced by the climbers until the idea of a fall was no longer dreadful. The second was a protection device for pitonless pitch—the expansion bolt.

Although expansion bolts had been used in Yosemite as early as the 19th century, their use had long been opposed (and still is) by the bulk of mountaineers. A common argument is that expansion bolts enable anyone to climb anything with ease, an argument that falls apart in view of the time and effort required to place a single bolt. Moreover, the RCS members were using the bolts primarily as protection devices, rather than as aid placements, in preparation for which they had practiced taking test falls of more than ten feet onto bolts at their practice area in Berkeley. It is also a tribute to the skill of the RCS members that they placed only four bolts on the climb, a number that was increased significantly by those who were to repeat their route.

The RCS members—David Brower,stor Robineggnnnd John Dyer—examined the scene of Orme's fall and then prudently decided on another route; going up the west side, crossing to the east, and proceeding to the summit. On the first day, they used an improvised rope-and-carabiner "elevator" to pass an approach section and ended at the foot of a 30-foot double overhang. The foursome called a halt and went to dinner, courtesy of Mrs. Robinson. The next day they started into the overhanging pitch, where, even with the use of bolts, one day's climbing yielded only 12 feet of gain. On the third day the party returned equipped for a bivouac and finished the overhang, and on the fourth day they reached the top after an exciting key pitch which required the use of a lasso to gain a crucial horn. Shiprock, regarded as the most challenging rock climb in North America, was made just a tiny bit taller by a summit cairn and a Sierra Club register.

Once climbed, Shiprock became known as a desert

classic all over America. Repeat ascents and new routes were established, including Bill Forrest's Grade VI route on the "impossible" East Face. This climbing tradition was cut short in April 1970 when, to the shock and surprise of climbers throughout the world, Shiprock was closed to climbing by the Navaho tribe, owners of the site. The closure came after many parties had failed to register climbing plans properly with the Navaho tribal council, and it was supported by tribal groups who felt that climbing desecrated the religious significance of Tsae-bid-tae. On March 27, 1970, a weather-related climbing accident necessitated the evacuation of an injured climber from the rock. The publicity of the accident and the expense of the rescue motivated the Navaho tribe to close the rock to all climbers but those with written permission from the Navaho authorities. The closure was made complete one year later, when the Navaho imposed an unconditional ban against camping and climbing in the Shiprock area.

Although this ban may seem unreasonable to many climbers, it must be realized that for the Navaho people Shiprock has a special significance that far precedes the first mountaineering attempts on it. Moreover, the ban was put into effect after more than 30 years of Navaho experience with allowing climbers to use the area, and it cannot, therefore, be called a blind ban against climbing.

It can only be hoped that at some time in the near future the dependability and responsibility of rock climbers will persuade the Navaho tribal council that such climbers are worthy of making the ascent to the tips of the Great Stone Bird's wings.

References

Anderson, Ernie. "Navahos Close Shiprock." *Summit*, May 1970, pp. 18-19.

Anderson, Ernie. "Shiprock: Permanent Climbing Ban." *Summit*, June 1971, p. 1.

Brower, David R. "It Couldn't Be Climbed." *Saturday Evening Post*, 3 February 1940, pp. 24–25+.

Clark, Ronald W. *Men, Myths, and Mountains*. London: Weidenfeld and Nicolson, 1976. P. 160.

Forrest, Bill. Letter of December 1977.

Jones, Chris. *Climbing in North America*. Berkeley: University of California Press for American Alpine Club, 1976. Pp. 107–41.

Ormes, Robert M. "A Piece of Bent Iron." *Saturday Evening Post*, 22 July 1939, pp. 13+.

14

The Titan

American rock climbers are notoriously fond of hard rock. The polished walls of Yosemite are glacially finished granite, and the popular areas in the East are gritstone or some other quartz-hard rock. The well-known walls in the Rockies are uplifted granite blocks. American technique and technology have been built around a tradition of bombproof holds on solid rock.

With this in mind, take, if you will, a shaft of soft red sandstone some 900 feet tall. File and shape it so that it looks more like a vertical airfoil than a rock formation. Give it as few cracks as possible, and then spray the whole thing with a coating of mud several inches thick. Finally, just for good measure, plant a desert around it. The creation described, give or take a few overhangs, would be the Titan, the tallest member of the Fisher Towers group of eastern Utah. Few rock climbing problems more improbable could be imagined.

It is only human for one's mind to wander while working, and one day, while working on the Colorado Plateau for the U.S. Geological Survey, Huntley Ingalls found

The Fisher Towers group stands in contrast to the distant La Sal Mountains. (Photo by Don Briggs, courtesy George Hurley)

himself contemplating the Titan with the competent eye of an experienced rock climber. He knew from USGS experience that the mud surface of the Fisher Towers was backed up by reasonably solid sandstone. That was hope enough. He began to form a plan for climbing the Titan.

Ingalls started by contacting Layton Kor, the Boulder, Colorado, climber who had gained the respect of climbers the world over for his competent manner and excellent technique on difficult rock problems. Kor had done extensive desert and soft-rock climbing and was an expert on climbing less-than-desirable faces.

Then George Hurley was added to the team. When not teaching English at the University of Colorado, Hurley could often be found with Kor at Eldorado Springs Canyon or one of the other Boulder crags. Together, Kor and Hurley had done the first ascent of the *Grand Giraffe*, which, despite the humorous overtones of its name, was (and is) an outstandingly difficult climb, with a crux crack rated at 5.9. The two had also made short work of the *McCarthy West Face* route on Devils Tower, finishing the

The Titan. (Photo by
George Hurley)

route (5.8, A2) in only six hours, a very good time for a
six-pitch aid route done with pitons. Kor had also been
active with Ingalls, having climbed Castle Rock (only six
miles from the Titan) with Ingalls in 1961. It was a strong
team.

The three climbers put a great deal of thought and time
into the preparation for their 1962 attempt. They made a
practice climb on the Bell Tower (also known as the
Kissing Couple) in Colorado National Monument. A reconnaissance trip to the Titan showed the north side to be the
most promising. The threesome made a probe as far as the
Finger of Fate, a prominent gendarme on the Titan's side,
where they cached 14 quarts of water against future
needs. The probe showed that there were crack systems
under the mud all the way up to the Finger—a good sign,
as these permitted the use of pitons and thus made it
possible to cut down on the use of bolts.

The actual climb was postponed pending the arrival of
Barry Bishop, a *National Geographic* photographer who
had been assigned to photograph the climb for his maga-

A view from the north. This is the side that the first ascent party climbed. (Photo by George Hurley)

The Titan. Note the Finger of Fate, midway on the right skyline. (Photo by George Hurley)

zine. Bishop would not be dead weight; a member-to-be of the 1963 American Everest Expedition, he knew about climbing and would be able to help the team out.

One of Bishop's contributions was a cast-aluminum handle equipped with triggers and a toothed cam. The device had been invented by a Swiss government bird-bander who wanted a simple means of climbing ropes to reach eagles' nests. Bishop had picked up some of the handles in Switzerland, and he showed the climbers how they could be put on the rope, with etriers attached, and used to ascend fixed lines. Ingalls took to the new tools quickly, finding them a fast way to climb ropes. Hurley would not accept them. He writes, "I refused to use them, since they did not look solid enough to me. I used the Prusik knots I had always used."

The handles were called Jumars, and they were soon to achieve widespread use on big wall and multiday climbs, not only for rope-climbing, but also for sack-hauling, self-belays, and rescue work. Hurley's dubious reaction to them

Ray Jardine leads the Finger of
Fate traverse on a later Titan
ascent. (Photo by Bill Forrest)

may seem strange to the modern Yosemite climber, whose
Jumars are as much a part of his equipment as his
carabiners. It must be remembered, however, that his first
sight of the devices occurred on the eve of a first ascent
which already involved several unknowns. His decision to
rely on a proven and simple method was the honest
reaction of an experienced mountaineer.

At any rate, equipped with both Jumars and Prusik
slings, the three were ready for the Titan. An overflight in
a small plane had revealed some nasty-looking summit
overhangs. Once the three climbers were on the rock, the
crux proved to be the Finger of Fate traverse, an "exposed, overhung, and rotten" around-the-corner journey
with dubious protection (the quoted description is George
Hurley's). Once the Finger was passed, the route settled
down to nothing more than difficult and highly exposed
mixed climbing on the strange soft rock to which the three
climbers were now growing accustomed.

The climb went smoothly for the next two pitches, after

which the cracks ran out. Bolts were then resorted to. This proved slow going, and the team bivouacked on a ledge. There, the three passed a difficult night, exposed to the wind and the cold desert air on a ledge that was too small for comfort.

The next day, the trio arose to make their summit bid. They had left fixed ropes up to the bivouac ledge. Now, though their supply of rope was ample to fix the tower, they climbed without fixing lines. They expected a rough aid pitch, and time was of the essence. Luckily, they soon ran into another section of cracks. They made good time, and Kor lived up to his reputation as he spidered his way through the overhung summit girdle. Finally, protected by bolts, he pulled the last overhang, and Ingalls and Hurley Prusiked up to join him. Together, the three scrambled to the true summit of the Titan.

All told, the route had taken five days, one bivouac, and nine leads. It was rated at Grade V, 5.8, A3. About 20 percent of the route went free, but after George Hurley made the second ascent four years later, with T. M. Herbert and Tom Condon, he reported that the mud had not "grown back" where it had been chipped off and that the prefixed protection of the bolts made free climbing more promising. This cleared the way for climbers such as Roger Briggs to free the crux traverse and much of the route above the bivouac ledge. The Titan has since yielded one other route, the *Sun Devil*, on the south side. The original north side route is unnamed.

The Titan climb had a far-reaching effect on American climbing. It introduced Jumars, and it brought to light in a singularly dramatic style a type of climbing that was not taken directly from the Europeans. Soon, desert tower climbing was to come into its own for Western climbers, becoming for them what sea-cliff climbing was for climbers in Wales—a treasured specialty. The Titan climbers remained at the front of the desert wave. Kor continued to climb soft rock until his retirement from climbing, and Hurley is still making first ascents on towers in Colorado and Utah. One of his favorites is the Doric Column, a beautifully steep and symmetrical pillar in the Mystery Towers, east of the Fisher Towers group. George is enthusiastic about desert climbing. He says, "Desert climbing is unusual in this country in that it still offers first ascents to real summits." For those who claim that rock climbing is a frontierless sport, this is fresh and hearty food for thought.

References

Carter, Harvey T. "King Fisher." *Climbing*, no. 3 (September 1970), pp. 6–13.

Hurley, George. "Mystery Towers." *Climbing*, no. 3 (September 1970), pp. 15–17.

Hurley, George. Letter of December 1977.

Ingalls, Huntley. "We Climbed Utah's Skycraper Rock." *National Geographic*, November 1962, pp. 705–21.

Jones, Chris. *Climbing in North America*. Berkeley: University of California Press for American Alpine Club, 1976. P. 292.

Part 4
Big Walls

Throughout the history of climbing, part of the attraction of the sport has been its scale. The sheer dominating immensity of the peak is a significant factor in the worth and rewards of mountaineering. Much of rock climbing lacks this facet of climbing. A 400-foot rock climb may be exposed, but unlike a mountain it cannot shrink a climber to gnatlike proportions. In this respect, big wall climbing falls between rock climbing and mountaineering.

A big wall is a vertical challenge that demands sophisticated rock climbing technique and garners at least Grade V and often Grade VI ratings. Although big wall climbing was first done in Europe, it was only after Americans took up the sport that it began to grow to its present level of sophistication.

All things considered, American big wall climbing presents the greatest challenges that a rock climber can face today. Climbers in the Yosemite Valley have developed long climbs involving moves rated at the previously unheard of 5.12 level, and continuous refinements of ethics and technique are going on in these bizarre environments where few things, if any, are horizontal. Yosemite techniques and standards have spread throughout the country and through American climbers to big walls throughout the world.

In some paradoxical way it is good for man to feel small and vulnerable from time to time. To do the improbable and to feel, cold and thin, one's mortality, is to realize the gift of life fully. It is small wonder, therefore, that so many climbers are poets, musicians, and artists. Such people require unique insight into the human condition and a big wall can be the source of such insight. A big wall evokes the spirit within, drawing it forth by titanic challenges.

15

Half Dome

To modern American rock climbers, the Yosemite Valley has a standing somewhere above paradise and below heaven, and to many who are now entering the sport, Yosemite climbers are placed in a status just above the Communion of Saints and just below God. For the rock climber, out of all the valleys, cliffs, and crags of America, this is The Place—the crucible of 20th century American rock climbing.

The Yosemite Valley is beautiful, incredibly so, and it is its beauty which draws millions of visitors to Yosemite National Park each year. The Yosemite's beauty is also important to the rock climber—aesthetic appeal is a deeply ingrained but rarely measured part of rock climbing. But the main attraction of Yosemite to the rock climber is a basic ingredient of its total beauty—the great big walls of Yosemite granite.

The story of the Yosemite Valley's creation is well known. Like the Teton Range, the Sierra Nevada is the product of block-faulting, and, like the Tetons, the Yosemite Valley is the product of both stream erosion and glacial

Yosemite Valley's Half Dome. (Courtesy National Park Service)

action. The rock of the Yosemite Valley, however, is not like that of the Tetons.

The Yosemite big walls are made of an extremely smooth-surfaced granite. Like Cathedral Ledge and the other New Hampshire cliffs, the Yosmite walls are largely the product of exfoliation—a process in which slabs of rock, like the rings of a dried-out tree trunk, fall away to reveal the new rock beneath.

One of the better examples of the exfoliation process is a formation so familiar that many consider it to be the signature of the Yosemite Valley. This is Half Dome—a great and graceful granite peak whose name is perfectly descriptive. It is perhaps the most-photographed rock formation in the United States. The back and sides of Half

Half Dome as seen from the
national park's shuttle bus
route. (Courtesy National Park
Service)

Dome clearly illustrate the exfoliation process, with great
slabs of granite, called spalls, lying in perfectly parallel
layers on the curves of the great rock. This process has
produced the wide cracks and chimneys for which the
Yosemite Valley has become known—surprisingly uniform
and incredibly smooth.

Half Dome's most famous feature, its broad and flat
dead-vertical Northwest Face, is the subject of much
confusion among valley visitors. Many of these visitors
assume that Half Dome is a dome which was sanded in
half by glacial action, but in reality it was formed by a
less romantic process. The flat face is the product of
exfoliation along natural weaknesses in the rock, and
surprisingly enough, there never was another half to Half
Dome. This will come as a letdown to some people, but it
certainly hasn't hurt the climbing any.

The Yosemite Valley came to public attention in the
mid-19th century, largely through the action of the California Geological Survey. While working for the Survey,
Clarence King mapped and ascended all of the major
points in the valley, with the exception of Half Dome,
which he pronounced totally unclimbable. The valley grew

Half Dome the easy way, via
the cable route following the
old Anderson line. Note the
slabs typical of exfoliated
granite. (Photo by Pat Bessner)

in popularity, but through the conservation actions in-
voked by John Muir, it was spared from commercial
exploitation. At this time, there were several attempts to
climb Half Dome. The most persistent attempts were
made by a Scottish carpenter named George Anderson,
who experimented with using tar as an adhesive to aid
him in barefooted pioneer friction climbing. Finally, in
1875, Anderson managed to reach the summit by ascending the curved side of the peak with the aid of a rope and
iron eyes in drilled holes. Thus Anderson became the first
man to climb Half Dome, while also acquiring the dubious
honor of being the first climber to place a bolt in the
Yosemite Valley.

The National Park Service soon overhauled Anderson's
route up the Northeast Face of Half Dome, putting in
cable handrails and regular bracing-steps. This made it
possible for just about anyone to climb to the summit, and
thousands of park visitors have since done so. Yet for years
this was the only way to the top. The age of Yosemite
climbing was yet to come.

In 1946, it was the Southwest Face of Half Dome that
was intriguing Yosemite Valley climbers. Higher Cathe-

dral Spire had been climbed, and the Lost Arrow had been topped out as well, albeit by dubious means. These victories had given Yosemite climbers new confidence, and the improbable Southwest Face now seemed possible.

The first ascent of Half Dome had been made by a Scottish carpenter. Now, it was a Swiss blacksmith who hoped to make his mark at Half Dome.

John Salathe was not like most of the valley climbers. For one thing, he was older, a middle-aged man in a sport dominated by youths in their twenties. For another thing, he was not the wild, fast-living, and careless type that had come to be associated with American rock climbing. Salathe was a serious, workmanlike person, a vegetarian and a nondrinker. He trained for his climbing both mentally and physically, and he thought of rock climbing as a tonic for the psyche.

Salathe looked at the Southwest Face as a good thing to do, rather than as a challenge or a bold frontier. With Ax Nelson, he planned the route and readied for the climb. The pair had several things going for them. They were both committed climbers, and they both took physical conditioning seriously. They trusted each other's abilities, and they were able to assess dangers and to deal with them. Also, like the carpenter Anderson, who had used his occupational skills to conquer Half Dome, the blacksmith Salathe was to use his trade to his advantage.

On earlier Yosemite climbs, Salathe had watched with dismay as his soft pitons bent and mushroomed when he tried to force them into small Yosemite cracks. Familiar with the properties of steel, he looked for a way to make a better piton. He found the harder steel he needed in a scrap automobile axle, and made pitons from it. The new pitons worked well in the granite, and could be removed and redriven over and over again. By the time Salathe got to Half Dome, he was confident in his pitons, the design of which is now a standard for pitons the world over. Salathe and Nelson went up the Southwest Face, bivouacked, and finished their climb the next day. They descended by the cable route, rejoicing in the knowledge that they had not come up that way.

Ten years later, the big wall portion of Half Dome had become the target. Steep, wide, and ominous, the 2,000-foot Northwest Face, with its aura of impenetrability, was calling American rock climbing to come of age. Answering this call were Royal Robbins, whose name has been synonymous with the sport of rock climbing; and Warren "Batso" Harding, whose name has been synonymous with lechery. Robbins was a serious climber who developed bouldering moves into a new level of lead climbing, and Harding was a longtime valley climber who scoffed at the aura of sanctity that climbing was developing, referring to Yosemite as a "gymnasium." The two were different in their views but very much alike in their ability to climb at the highest standards. Their party pushed a three-day attempt toward the summit of the steep face, but came down when it was obvious that the face would take more time and preparation.

In 1957, Robbins returned with another party, and after five days of coping with unprecedented difficulties, not the least of which was the sheer scale of the climb, he led his party to the top. It was a first for America, a Grade VI.

In the following years, Yosemite climbing began to accelerate. In 1966 Eric Beck soloed Robbins' route on the Northwest Face of Half Dome, and by 1973 this route had been done using chocks only. In 1976, Jim Erickson and Art Higbee freed all but the last pitch of this route. They later returned to top-rope the final pitch free and fix protection bolts. This made the entire climb free, although it has not been led that way as of this writing. Purists will delight at a bit of trivia concerning the Erickson-Higbee attempt: neither of them used chalk, although the climbing was at the 5.11 level.

Once Robbins had put a route on Half Dome's vertical face, it seemed necessary for him to own the face. The original route, the *Northwest Face Route*, was to the left side of the wall, where the rock was more broken. In 1969,

Royal Robbins and Don Peterson pushed a bold new route—called *Tis-sa-ack*—up the middle of the Northwest Face. The blankness in the center was overcome by using bolts, a tedious chore compounded by an overlong drill holder and drill bits equally overlong. The route took eight days and was rated Grade VI, 5.9, A4.

By 1971, there were four routes on Half Dome's distinctive Northwest Face—the *Northwest Face Route*, *Arcturus*, *Northwest Face Direct*, and *Tis-sa-ack*. All of those routes had been pioneered by Royal Robbins.

Half Dome is an excellent example of the progress American rock climbing has made in the last century. First climbed by a carpenter with little knowledge of the ways of mountaineering, it next succumbed to a blacksmith who knew how to rock-climb as well as how to work steel. Then, as the standards advanced, it was time for a new breed of rock climbing specialist who could combine strength, skill, imagination, and determination to push the thresholds of the sport even farther.

Big wall climbing had its beginnings in the Alps, and to a great extent it was developed in the Dolomites. It was at Yosemite, however, that big wall climbing advanced to its present stage. At the core of this advance was Half Dome.

References

Clark, Ronald W. *Men, Myths, and Mountains*. London: Weidenfeld and Nicolson, 1976. Pp. 44–45, 217, 244, and 248.

Evans, Tom. "Half Dome." *Summit*, May 1973, pp. 27-28.

Gerhardt, Clark. "Yosemite Valley." *Mountain*, no. 52 (November/December 1976), p. 14.

Higgins. "Yosemite." *Mountain*, no. 51 (September/October 1976), p. 14.

Jones, Chris. *Climbing in North America*. Berkeley: University of California Press for American Alpine Club, 1976. Pp. 26, 207–11, 355, and 367–69.

Matthews, William H. III. *A Guide to the National Parks.* Garden City, N.Y.: Natural History Press, 1968. Vol. 1, pp. 377–88.

Robbins, Royal. "Arcturus—A New Route on Half Dome." *Summit,* April 1971, pp. 5–7.

Robbins, Royal. "Tis-sa-ack." *Mountain,* no. 18 (November 1971), pp. 21–25.

Rowell, Galen. "Twenty-Five Days South Face of Half Dome." *Summit,* December 1970, pp. 2–9.

Scott, Doug. *Big Wall Climbing.* New York: Oxford University Press, 1974. Pp. 143–45, 158, and 241.

16

El Capitan

Half Dome was a prelude to the golden age of Yosemite, during which the big wall climb became a refined and polished Yosemite Valley art form. On the Northwest Face, climbers had tasted the overwhelming verticality and isolation that would soon become standard fare in the valley. *Tis-sa-ack*, the line of which had been thought of by dozens of climbers as the Ultimate Climb, had been done. It was time to seek new horizons. It was time for El Capitan.

In the mid-50s, El Cap had only one route, the *East Buttress*. This was very much a prelude route, good for its day, but not in the same league as Robbins' lines on Half Dome. Warren Harding, who had arrived in the Valley just days too late to capture the first ascent of Half Dome's Northwest Face, was looking for something else to climb. Like all good climbers, Harding was blessed with a Grade A ego, and he made up his mind to do something one cut above the *Northwest Face Route*. Looking around the valley for a suitable route, he decided, with the help of liberal quantities of Mountain Red wine, to do the South Buttress of El Capitan.

El Capitan stands thousands of feet above the Yosemite Valley. Note Half Dome in the distant center. (Courtesy National Park Service)

The South Buttress, or Nose, of El Capitan is a 3,000-foot curve of granite which starts out in a very steep grade and soon relinquishes itself to verticality, with generous amounts of overhang for variety. The scale of the Nose is simply phenomenal. Done in a perfectly straight line, with no rope slack or traverses whatsoever, it would still require more than 20 pitches of climbing. It is a south-facing route that makes the idea of "fun in the California sun" seem like a bad joke, and the scarcity of spacious ledges on the climb is highly conducive to cases of big-wall fever, the climbing version of cabin fever.

But Harding wanted the Nose. In scale, he reasoned, the South Buttress of El Capitan was the rock climbing equivalent of the mountaineer's Mount Everest, so he decided to use tactics similar to those of a major Himalayan expedition in the attempt. This meant siege climbing, with all of the equipment investment and logistic problems it involved. Assisting Harding were Mark Powell and Bill Feuerer, a mechanical genius nicknamed "the Dolt."

The team ascended the buttress in spurts. The team would climb for days at a time, then descend on fixed ropes to rest, regroup, return to their jobs, and plan the next pitches. Weeks went by. Powell broke his ankle during a recess from the climbing, requiring corrective surgery which hampered his climbing technique. The Dolt withdrew from the effort after seriously contemplating the scale of the route and deciding that the climbers would be pushing things too close to the thin edge of their abilities. The superintendent of Yosemite National Park was growing a bit impatient, and the crowds of spectators watching the climbers were growing larger with each new effort. New climbers were continually drafted by Harding, and by the time the route had been pushed to Boot Flake, he was the only remaining member of the original team. His new partners were George Whitmore and Wayne Merry. The equipment collections of a number of valley climbers had been borrowed to facilitate the climb, and a number of equipment innovations had been tried on it, including a hauling cart for bringing up equipment (which didn't work too well) and oversized pitons made from stove legs (which worked quite well). Visiting climbers stopped by at the route site, put in their time at hauling gear and fixing lines, and moved on. It began to seem that the *Nose Route* would never end.

Finally, 18 months after making the first moves to plan his route, Warren Harding finished it, at a little past five in the morning on November 12, 1958. A total of a month and a half had been devoted to actual climbing, with unbroken stretches of up to 12 days spent on the wall. The man-hours involved were never computed, but the number had to be astronomical. It was a climb of huge proportions.

The *Nose Route* drew criticism corresponding to its scale. Climbers said that the route had been "gang-banged" rather than climbed, and pointed out that a vertical gain of just a little more than 66 feet per day was hardly an impressive track record. The national park officials expressed concern about the pitons that had been left in the route, and the leaders of the sport voiced their chagrin when members of the first ascent party expressed their intentions of profiting from the climb by writing and lecturing about it. Harding listened to it all, unruffled. He had made the first ascent of the Nose, and nothing could change that.

Harding's route was repeated two years later by Royal Robbins, Tom Frost, Chuck Pratt, and Joe Fitscher without the use of siege tactics—in one great push. Done this way, the climb took a week. Undoubtedly, the fact that many of the bolts and pitons necessary for the climb were already there contributed to this remarkably improved time, but it was the lightweight alpine-style technique which did the most to speed up the climbing. Big wall climbing was already becoming refined.

Subsequent accomplishments on the *Nose Route* show the continuing refinement of Yosemite Valley climbing.

The third ascent of the route, by Layton Kor, Glen Denny, and Steve Roper, cut the time to just over three days. In 1973, the route was climbed by Yvon Chouinard and Bruce Carson without hammers or pitons, using only chocks and fixed pegs. Dennis Henneck and Don Lauria climbed the Nose in 2½ days, and Tom Bauman soloed it in 1969. In 1972, climbers were sufficiently familiar and comfortable with the South Buttress to effect a rescue of Neal Olsen, who had broken his leg 2,000 feet up the face. In 1975, Jim Bridwell, Billy Westbay, and John Long

The Yosemite Valley from Artist's Point. El Capitan is to the left. (Courtesy National Park Service)

speed-climbed the Grade VI route in 15 hours, starting at 4 A.M. and finishing the night off in a Yosemite-area bar. Today, only a small fraction of the route is done with aid.

With the South Buttress climbed, El Capitan was open for the new-route business. The *Salathe Wall*, perhaps the most natural big wall line on El Cap, was done in two pushes by Robbins, Frost, and Pratt in 1961. During the next two years the *Dihedral Wall* and the *West Buttress* were established, followed by the *Muir Wall* in 1965. Possibly the most significant of the climbs made at this time was the *North America Wall*, which Chouinard, Frost, Pratt, and Robbins climbed in nine days in 1964 with less than 40 bolts. The route, which goes up the West Coast side of a dark spot on the wall resembling a map of North America, had some of the most demanding free climbing and the most delicate aid of any yet done on an American big wall. The route's rating was Grade VI, 5.8, A5, respectable enough on a crag climb and almost unbelievable on a big wall.

Harding greeted the '70s with fuel for yet another El

Capitan controversy, by doing a climb called the *Wall of the Early Morning Light* (the *Dawn Wall*). Valley climbers saw nothing of beauty in this climb but its name. As on his pioneer '50s climb of El Capitan, Harding had arranged for as much publicity as possible and hoped to profit from the climb by writing and lecturing. Even more upsetting to the natives were Harding's tactics. He used bolts freely, placing more than 300 of them to create a route across absolutely blank sections of rock. In a 180° reversal of his old siege-climbing tactics, Harding, with his partner, Dean Caldwell, made the climb in one push, although the "push" lasted almost a month. The press crowded the park and filled tons of newsprint with talk of drama on the cliffs. After the climbers had been on the wall 20 days, the National Park Service came to the conclusion that they had gone out of their minds from the exposure and were never coming down. A rescue was organized, and Harding, slightly intoxicated on a bivouac ledge, chased away the Good Samaritans with screamed obscenities. Finally, 27 days after starting, the pair pulled over the top and were pounced on by the media. The climbing journals howled with outrage; Robbins started to chop the bolts out of the wall; and the American climbing community started debates, not yet concluded, over whether Harding should be commended for bravery or shot.

Today, El Capitan is a continuing showplace for all that is new and innovative in American big-wall climbing. It is climbed by members of both sexes. An all-woman ascent of the *Triple Direct* route in 1973 proved that women could do everything required in climbing as well as men, with the single exception of sack-hauling (the climbers were not heavy enough for effective pulleying). Soloing has become more common, with self-belays and mechanical Prusik brakes being refined to acceptable levels, and the emphasis is now on free climbing in the cleanest style possible. El Capitan remains a colorful example of Yosemite history, and though this has nothing whatsoever to do with climbing, it seems fitting to note here that in 1972 Rick

Two views of El Capitan.
(Photo by Pat Bessner)

Sylvester *skied* off the top of El Cap, opening a parachute at the last moment to prevent himself from becoming a small splotch on the valley floor.

Climbers planning to visit Yosemite would be wise to look through Steve Roper's *Climber's Guide to Yosemite Valley*, as it answers most of the obvious questions. Yosemite is a national park, and this means that climbs must be registered and that the valley will be quite crowded, particularly in the summer.

It is important for climbers to realize that although Yosemite routes are being done cleaner, freer, and faster each year, this is because the climbers are getting better, not because the routes are getting any easier. In short, the *Nose Route* is not the place to learn about upper-grade climbing, and those who get into predicaments on routes because they are not up to the climbing required should not feel that they have the right to bolt their way past the hard parts. Climbers should climb within their limits and practice Jumaring, load-hauling, bivouacking, wall rescue, and other needed skills *before* turning themselves loose on the valley walls. They should also be aware that California is not all sunshine and that bivouac gear and foul-weather gear, as well as a continuously planned retreat route, are necessities on all wall routes, since blind foolishness and lack of preparation for storms account for far too many rescues.

Between 1972 and 1977, the National Park Service has been called upon to provide 115 rescues or searches per annum for valley climbers. This ridiculously high number of rescues is obviously due to a lack of foresight on the part of many climbers who want to be Yosemite veterans without investing the necessary effort in conditioning, training, and planning. Questions about routes or procedures can be addressed to park climbing rangers, and to be on the safe side, climbers may want to pay a visit to the *Yosemite Mountaineering School*. The valley is neither vicious nor a death trap, but it is a place of high-standard rock climbing in breathtaking surroundings, and it deserves consideration by its visitors.

References

Burton, Hugh. "El Capitan Up-date." *Mountain*, no. 44 (July/August 1975), pp. 24–30.

Clark, Ronald W. *Men, Myths, and Mountains*. London: Weidenfeld and Nicolson, 1976. Pp. 222–23, 244–48.

Evans, Tom. "On El Capitan." *Summit*, June 1972, pp. 22–25.

Haan, Peter. "The Salathe Wall Solo." *Summit*, November/December 1971, pp. 24–27.

Hechtal, Sibylle. "All-Woman Climb of El Capitan." *Summit*, April 1974, pp. 6–9.

Jones, Chris. *Climbing in North America.* Berkeley: University of California Press for American Alpine Club, 1976. Pp. 196, 267–83, and 371.

Robbins, Royal. "The El Capitan Climb." *Summit*, December 1970, pp. 30–31.

Scott, Doug. *Big Wall Climbing.* New York: Oxford University Press, 1974. Pp. 144, 146–54, and 156–62.

Thompson, Pete. "Rescue on El Capitan." *Summit*, October 1972, pp. 1–3.

Anonymous. "Yosemite Rescue." *Mountain*, no. 29 (September 1973), pp. 39–41.

17

The Diamond
of Long's Peak

At 14,255 feet, Long's Peak is the highest peak in the Rocky Mountain National Park area. It is also by far the most popular peak in the area. Although the summit lies more than seven miles away from, and almost 5,000 feet above, the nearest parking lot, it remains a popular spot with tourists, and several thousand visit it each year. Formerly, two routes were available for nontechnical ascents—the *Cables*, named for a steep stretch on the North Face which was rigged with steel cable to aid hikers, and the *Keyhole Route*, a longer route which was used as a descent route by hikers and climbers alike. In 1973, in keeping with the wilderness designation of the area, the cable was removed from the North Face, and that route reverted to the 5.3 it had been some 40-odd years before. All nontechnical traffic then shifted to the *Keyhole*, but despite this change the peak has gained in popularity with hikers.

The summit of Long's attracts a weird mixture of people. It has been climbed by toddlers and octogenarians, and wedding ceremonies have been performed at the

151

summit register. The peak has been ascended on crutches, and a brass sextet is reported to have climbed it and given a concert at the summit in the late 19th century. On one Saturday in August, I counted better than 25 people lounging about at the Keyhole Pass, for which the route is named, and literally dozens more were passing up and down the trail to the summit with antlike regularity. Long's Peak is a popular mountain.

Yet it is a mountain with two personalities.

On its East Face the prospect is quite different. Here the *hoi polloi* are conspicuously lacking, for on this side the routes are technical, the faces are steep, and the atmosphere is less amiable. The East Face rises 2,000 feet above Chasm Lake, with small glaciers and snow tongues guarding its approaches. High on its upper half, above a dividing ledge known as Broadway, is a steep subface about 900 feet high and 1,000 feet wide, shaped like a rough square standing on one corner. This is the Diamond—the most important alpine wall in the state of Colorado.

Long's, the 15th highest peak in Colorado, was first climbed by the Ute, who trapped eagles on its summit. The first recorded ascent was made in 1868, by a party led by the Grand Canyon explorer John Wesley Powell. The Powell party made their climb via the *Homestretch*, which is now the latter part of the *Keyhole* route. It was not until three years later that a climber set foot on the East Face. Oddly enough, he did it from the top down.

His name was Elkanah J. Lamb, and he was a minister by occupation and a mountain walker by avocation. In 1871, he walked up the *Keyhole* to the summit, where, concluding that he had already seen what the *Keyhole* had to offer, he decided to take another way down. The other way he took was the East Face, steep, unexplored, and certainly a tall order for a lone and unequipped hiker. Lamb made his way down the face to the upper tongue of Mills Glacier, where the odds caught up with him and he slipped on the ice and fell, out of control. A fall at that

The Diamond, East Face of Long's Peak, from Chasm View. (Photo by Bruce Groves)

spot can be quite serious, as was the case in 1968, when a climber who fell there struck his head on the rocks below, his life saved only by emergency brain surgery in the Chasm Lake Shelter Cabin. Lamb, however, managed to grab an outcrop after sliding a good distance down the tongue. Today, the place where he fell is known as Lamb's Slide. This was the extent of East Face mountaineering until 1906, when Enos Mills, a Long's Peak guide and a naturalist, followed Lamb's route, again from the top to the bottom.

Finally, in 1923, a Princeton professor named J. W. Alexander made the inevitable move and climbed Lamb's route from the bottom to the top.

The East Face attracted climbers from time to time after 1915, when the area became part of Rocky Mountain National Park. In 1927, Joe and Paul Stettner climbed *Stettner's Ledges* (5.7) on the lower part of the face, to the left of the Diamond, opening the face to upper-level rock climbing. This route was an indication of great things to come, such as the ascent of the *Diagonal* (5.9, A3), by Layton Kor and Ray Northcutt in 1959, which proved to be the first Grade V in Colorado.

The Diamond, however, was still a virgin face. This was due, not to a lack of contenders, but to a lack of opportunity. The National Park Service had declared the Diamond off limits to technical climbing, on the ground that it would be difficult or impossible to mount a rescue should a party become incapacitated on the face. Finally, in 1960, the Diamond was opened to climbing on the condition that the climbing parties were to be supported by backup teams, in the event that a rescue should become necessary. Permits to make climbs were sent to those who had requested them, and Dave Rearick and Bob Kamps, two California climbers, were among the first to receive them. They hastily organized things, and in July and August of that year, they established *D-1*, the first route on the Diamond.

D-1 (V, 5.7, A4) quickly became known around Colorado as a fierce climb. So did the next five routes on the wall, and Diamond climbers took it as a fact of life that any new route on the wall would have at least one pitch that would scare the daylights out of them.

The Diamond—a big wall high
in Colorado's Front Range.
(Photo by Don Briggs, courtesy
Bill Forrest)

In 1966, George Hurley, Wayne Goss, and Larry Dalke
approached the Diamond with a new route in mind. As
they hiked toward the East Face, each of them wondered
what new terror the Diamond had in store for them.
Hurley recalls:

> The day we started D-7, the east face of Long's was com-
> pletely covered with thick cloud. There were four of us who
> went up to do the route; one person turned back because of
> the appearance of the weather. I had spent a summer in the
> European Alps, and I had the usual Alpine philosophy: "Get
> in position when the weather is bad, and go for it when the
> clouds break." Still, I was nervous because of the steepness.

The "Alpine philosophy" paid off. Two pitches were fixed
above Broadway, and the climbers bivouacked at the base
of their climb. The next day brought fair weather and
good climbing to Table Ledge, a horizontal feature which
crosses the entire Diamond. The climbers spent a comfortable night on the ledge, and the next day a single pitch of

5.7 climbing brought them to the summit. When they had finished, they realized that they had pioneered a route which would soon become a classic. With a free move of no more than 5.7, and no aid beyond A2, *D-7* was the first Diamond route that approached the realm of normal climbing. Today it is the most popular route on the Diamond.

In the next few years the Diamond grew in popularity, and more climbers came to try the wall as those who had already climbed it worked on new routes. Hurley, no longer nervous over the steepness, put four more routes on the Diamond, and climbers from around the world came to log ascents.

This increase in Diamond traffic caused the National Park Service to relax Diamond regulations slightly. Backup parties were no longer necessary, and it became easier to receive permission to climb. Then, in 1970, the NPS went one step farther and decided to allow solo climbing in Rocky Mountain National Park. A new race was on to make the first solo ascent of the Diamond.

One of the persons intrigued by the lifting of the solo ban was Bill Forrest, a veteran Colorado climber and a mountaineering equipment manufacturer. His first impulse was to grab the solo as quickly as possible, but, sensibly, he waited:

> I would have attempted the solo earlier . . . if I had been prepared. I trained and prepared all spring and summer, and did not allow myself to attempt the wall until I was thoroughly prepared. The temptation to make the effort earlier to avoid losing the first solo was great.

Forrest's reasoning was sound. There were several attempts to solo the Diamond that spring, and all failed. In late July, Forrest felt ready to give the wall a try. Moreover, he had decided not only to solo the wall but also to do a new route. He would start the climb by doing the first three leads of the *Yellow Wall* and then break new ground.

Making his way to Broadway, Forrest fixed a self-belay

Bill Forrest's tension vanishes with a grin as he finishes the final pitch of the first solo of the Diamond in July 1970. (Photos by Don Briggs, courtesy Bill Forrest)

system using a Heddon knot, backed up by a Jumar when the situation warranted it. In theory, the knot would slide freely along the rope in normal climbing, but close on the rope if a sudden load was applied during a fall. The Jumar was simply insurance to make sure that practice followed theory. The knot was tied in one-inch webbing and fastened to Forrest's harness with a locking carabiner. Thus prepared, Forrest climbed the first four pitches and started making a new route at the end of the fourth lead. Here he bivouacked in his hammock, the wall above him, losing what little sleep he might have gotten when a rock slide thundered down the North Chimney, lighting the night with its sparks.

The next day was the test, as Forrest climbed new territory to Table Ledge. The climbing was difficult, and the pressure of making a first solo ascent was always present, but that evening Forrest knew he was in control of the climb. He passed a good night on the ledge and was on the summit by noon of the following day. *Forrest Finish* (V, 5.8, A3) had closed another Diamond frontier.

The Diamond is still a popular wall, offering high-standard climbing in an extraordinary alpine setting. *D-7* has been freed, at 5.10, and undoubtedly other routes will soon follow suit. As the space for new routes grows smaller and smaller, eliminating aid and limiting protection to nuts and fixed pins promise to add ample room for Diamond firsts.

Although national park authorities have greatly reduced the amount of red tape necessary to do a Diamond climb, it is still necessary to register before climbing, and all camping and bivouacs are by permit only.

The usual procedure for a Diamond climb is to hike to the Boulderfield, where one rappels from Chasm View to Broadway. The climbers generally fix ropes on one or two pitches before bivouacking on the ledge, and climbs not

Bill Forrest and his support team relax at the Long's Peak boulder field just after Forrest's first Diamond solo. Left to right: Gary Garbert, Bill Forrest, Don Briggs, and Leonard Sanders. (Photo by Brenda Garbert, courtesy Bill Forrest)

completed the next day usually involve bivouacs on Table Ledge, which is also an escape route for some climbs.

It should be remembered, however, that this is an alpine wall. The climbs all start above 13,000 feet, and climbers who have just come from sea level will have to give their bodies time to adjust. In general, lowlanders would do well to do the approach in steps, going only as far as Jim's Grove, at timberline, by the first night, to Boulderfield (12,760 feet) by the second, and on to Broadway on the third day. The routes are difficult enough, and it is not necessary to compound their difficulty with mountain sickness.

Helmets are a good idea, especially near the right side of the Diamond, and foul-weather gear is essential. The weather usually comes from the west, which is a blind side, and East Face conditions can go from sunny and mild to drizzle and whiteout in less than one minute. Afternoon thunderstorms are a regular event during the summer, with an ice storm hitting the wall afterward every now and then. Descent is by the *Keyhole* route, and at the Keyhole itself the Agnes Vaille shelter house, built in memory of a woman who died on the East Face, provides a refuge for climbers who are caught by storm on the descent.

References

Covington, Mike. "Diamond Commentary." *Mountain*, no. 40 (November 1974), pp. 17–20.

Crouch, Dee B. "Midwinter Rescue on Long's Peak." *Summit*, July/August 1969, pp. 8–11.

DuMais, Dick. "Rocky Mountains." *North American Climber*, November 1975, p. 9.

Eberhart, Perry, and Schmuck, Paul. *The Fourteeners*. Chicago: Swallow Press, 1970. Pp. 8–11.

Forrest, Bill. Letter of December 1977.

Fricke, Walter W. *A Climber's Guide to the Rocky Mountain National Park Area.* Boulder, Colo.: Walter W. Fricke, 1917. Pp. 76–79.

Fricke, Walter W. "Climbing at Rocky Mountain." *Off Belay,* no. 2 (April 1972), pp. 17–23.

Hurley, George. Letter of December 1977.

18

The Painted Wall

Colorado is a state most climbers associate with high mountains such as the Rockies or with sunwashed canyons such as the Boulder region. Yet Colorado climbing has other sides, sides seldom seen by the out-of-state visitor. Known to area climbers are such less familiar facets of Colorado climbing as Lizard Head Peak, with its scaly, rotten summit tower, and the desert towers of western Colorado. An even more bizarre facet of Colorado climbing exists in a narrow, deep gorge called the Black Canyon of the Gunnison River.

Frequented by Colorado climbers since the early 1930s, the Black Canyon, now a national monument, is famous for depth, for difficult and often brittle rock, and for extended climbing routes. Even getting to the base of Black Canyon climbs can be hazardous, since doing so involves descending steep, scree-filled gullies which have seemingly been designed to jangle a climber's nerves long before he begins his climb. The bottom of the canyon is quite narrow in places, effectively channeling rockfall from the heights into concentrated, hard-to-vacate spaces. And as if expo-

161

sure and rockfall were not bad enough, the canyon is home to a particularly hardy and effective breed of poison ivy which leaves many Black Canyon climbers literally itching to get off their climbs and back home to the comforts of calamine lotion. The rock is metamorphic granite, richly veined with light-colored pegmatite. Much Black Canyon rock has a well-deserved reputation for looseness.

Prior to the 1960s, Black Canyon climbers concentrated on prominent rock ribs which jutted from the walls and ran from river to rim. But as attention to big walls grew in Yosemite, and as Grade Vs became common on the Diamond, new interest was focused on the wide, virgin walls spanning the empty spaces between the regular Canyon rib climbs. The greatest of these prizes was the Painted Wall, a beautifully veined wall at the canyon's deepest spot, climbing nearly a half-mile from the river to the rim. It was little known, unclimbed, and best of all, it was long enough and looked difficult enough to merit a Grade VI classification, the first in Colorado.

At the lead in the movement to capture the Painted Wall was Layton Kor, who went after the wall the way he went after anything he took an interest in—with enthusiasm. He had an infectious drive for climbing new routes, and actually talked Pat Ament into attempting the Chasm View Wall of the canyon while Ament was recovering from a badly blistered pair of hands (caused by catching a Kor leader fall on the Bastille). Owing to the sorry condition of his second's hands, Kor was forced to retreat via a harrowing line, but he returned later the same year to bag the 1,600-foot, two-bivouac route with Jim McCarthy and Tex Bossier. Kor had climbed the aretes to both sides of the Painted Wall, carefully inspecting it on both ascents for route possibilities. In 1967, with Bob Culp and Larry Dalke, he decided to give the wall a go.

Kor's line, starting near the center of the wall, soon ran into the loose, peeling rock for which the Painted Wall has become famous. Soon the climb became a seemingly continuous aid pitch, on tenuous placements in a huge overhanging section of loose rock. A retreat was in order, and the trio backed off in a fashion as terrifying as the ascent. A later Kor attempt, with Dalke, proved just as fruitless. Yet another return to the Black Canyon, this time with Rusty Baillie, never got off the ground, since the Gunnison was in full spate, making it impossible to reach the base of the climb. Kor and Baillie continued to consider the wall awhile, during which time Kor's enthusiasm waned while Baillie's grew. Soon the baton was passed, and Baillie became the front-runner on the Painted Wall effort.

Baillie got in contact with Bill Forrest, owner of Forrest Mountaineering, Ltd., and started arrangements for a spring 1970 attempt on the Painted Wall. Forrest describes what ensued:

> Spring came, and Rusty had not contacted me. That winter he stopped by and said, "This spring for sure." I got ready for a spring '71 Painted Wall climb, but in April got a note from Rusty that he couldn't make it again. I decided that I wanted to do the Painted Wall . . . with another partner since Rusty just wasn't able to get away. But I didn't want to steal his route (Kor's route, too), so I looked for my own.

Though tied up in the spring, Baillie turned out to be free in the summer. In July 1971, he, Karl Karlstrom, and Scott Baxter went to work on Kor's old route. They hoped to bridge a blank 200-foot gap on the wall which separated a lower dihedral system from a "summit crack" which ran down 800 feet from the top, through two large pegmatite bands.

Four days of climbing put the three men at Layton Kor's old high point. Here they would have to begin the Stygian Traverse, the 200-foot route across the unknown to the base of the summit crack. Karlstrom, in the lead, did some delicate aid to a place where he could see across the traverse. It looked very bad, worse than they'd expected. A short discussion began. They had taken four days to reach a point that Kor had gained in just over two. They were tired, and the stay on the overhanging wall was beginning to have its effect. They decided to go back down.

The disappointing traverse and a hair-raising retreat did little to deter the climbers from trying again. They had, they reasoned, done a good portion of the route and taken a good, close look at the Stygian Traverse. They decided to return the following summer, to bring along an extra man in order to get the haul bags up faster, and to replan strategies for the long traverse to the summit crack. Other plans, however, were already under way.

Bill Forrest, who had been ready for two consecutive springs to try the Painted Wall, was not about to let another spring slip by without having a crack at it. He feltready, and his 1970 solo on the Diamond had built his confidence in his abilities. Kris Walker, Bill's business partner, had also soloed the Diamond, and the two had done a great deal of desert climbing together. They also trusted each other completely and were used to each other's company—a perfect team for a Grade VI climb.

Kris paid a visit to Black Canyon of the Gunnison National Monument, where, with a telephoto lens, he made a careful photographic study of the Painted Wall from the

The Painted Wall, in Colorado's Black Canyon of the Gunnison River. The *Forrest-Walker Route* is marked: the bottom circle shows the start of the route. The next circle is the site of the first two bivouacs. This is followed by the sites of the last two bivouacs and the finish. (Photo by Gene F. White, courtesy Bill Forrest)

South Rim of the canyon. Back in Denver, the shots were assembled into a large composite photograph which the men studied carefully for route possibilities. They chose a bold and direct line up the middle of the wall, to the left of Baillie's line. Cracks and dihedrals made most of the route look feasible, but ominous blank spots were crossed by the line as well. There seemed to be no way to navigate around the bald portions of the route, so the pair decided that they would just try to make their way through them. It seemed an impossible prospect—attempting an uncertain line up the toughest wall in Colorado with a two-man team where three-man teams had failed. Yet they decided to try. As Forrest wrote later:

> We knew that Layton and Rusty were good, and that they'd turned back several times. However, both Kris and I had soloed the Diamond. We figured we would climb until something stopped us. We were very confident of our own abilities.

So on an April Sunday in 1972 Bill Forrest and Kris Walker made their way down Sonuvabitch Gully with eight days' worth of food and supplies, ready for the Painted Wall. They were encouraged by the results of a two-day probe to the first blank spot indicated on the photos. A small crack at that spot led the way to more broken ground beyond. It looked as if the wall would go, so the pair descended in order to bring up the rest of their equipment and their bivvy gear.

That evening a snowstorm blanketed the canyon and bombed their campsite with rockfall. To make matters worse, Forrest had unwittingly tested the local poison ivy and had found it as potent as ever. The climb was suspended while the climbers waited for the weather to break and climbed out to visit a dermatologist.

Two days later, Forrest and Walker returned, hauled their gear up to their high point, and got on with it. What followed were five continuous days of gritty, hard climbing. The typical belayer's stance was to hunch close to the anchors, shoulders drawn as close as possible, staring down or into the rock, as innumerable chips of rock rattled his helmet. Forrest had assumed just such a stance when Walker, after a long runout, loosened a large block and found that he had no place to secure it. The rock was heavy, and Walker was losing his balance, so it had to go. With a shout to Forrest, Walker launched the block on what he hoped would be a path away from Forrest. Instead, it bounced straight at him. Forrest recalls:

> When the rock came, I was tied into my anchors so tightly that I couldn't move. It really looked like it was going to hit me, but it missed by an inch or so. This close call had me quite shaken for the next few hours . . . It's difficult to say that I had any reaction at all, other than fear.

Long after the ozone smell of breaking rock and the whistle of the rockfall had passed away, the pair continued to ponder their predicament. Invisible routes, snowstorms, poison ivy, and now guided-missile boulders. It was difficult to say what the Painted Wall would find to throw at them next.

What the wall had to throw at them next was a seemingly endless variety of difficult and sparsely protected leads. On the 17th pitch, Forrest watched as Walker pendulumed, then free-climbed over an overhang and out of sight, continuing without protection because there was no place to put it. This lead brought them to Death Valley, a steep gully covered with holds—all sloping the wrong way. It would take five leads to climb the gully alone.

Forrest says:

> The 24th pitch was the crux. The exposure, rope drag, and lack of protection were all incredible. The only anchor in the whole pitch that could have stopped a fall was the Lost Arrow that I drove in for the belay anchor.

This pitch under the huge summit roofs took five hours, and it required the only drilling used on the whole climb, a single, shallow hole for a bat hook. Then, one lead to the rope's end, and a shallow, rotten chimney gave way to the

Kris Walker on the crux 24th
pitch of the Painted Wall. (Photo
by Bill Forrest)

summit. After five days on the Painted Wall, Bill Forrest
and Chris Walker stepped onto the North Rim of the
Black Canyon. Colorado had its first Grade VI.

The Painted Wall (VI, 5.9, A4, 26 pitches, 4 bivouacs)
had gone half-free, half-aid, and without a bolt on the
route. The team had consisted of only two men, and nuts
had been used for aid and protection wherever possible. It
was not merely a route; it was a creation—a truly outstanding achievement. For the climbers, the summit
brought mixed feelings: "It was like getting out of jail, too.
We felt much relief and much satisfaction."

To Baillie, Karlstrom, Baxter, and their new team
member, David Lovejoy, the news was stunning. To hear
that the Painted Wall had been done at all was a blow, but
to hear that it had been done by a two-man team in five
days on a new route was crushing. The four climbers met
to decide whether to go on with their plans for a summer
'72 attempt. Baillie argued, in a variation of the old cliche,
that they had lost the wall but not the route. In June the
foursome returned to the Black Canyon, bolted, nutted,

and pinned across the Stygian Traverse, and finally, after much A4 work, reached the summit crack. From the base of the crack, it took them one day to reach the Lovely Bivouac Ledge, another day to reach the Buzzard's Roost, and a third day to get on top. Called *Dragon Route* after the dragonlike pegmatite bands crossed by the climb, this second Painted Wall route took nine days to climb, was 20 pitches in length, and like the first route, was graded VI, 5.9, A4.

Located about 70 miles southeast of Grand Junction, Colorado, the Black Canyon of the Gunnison National Monument offers climbing of extreme grades in an extraordinary setting. The unusual order of things, with the descent coming before the climb, can take some getting used to, and Black Canyon climbers are unanimous in their opinions as to the worth of hard hats in the canyon. The Painted Wall climbs proved that the sixth grade was not the exclusive property of the high mountains and the Yosemite Valley, and Forrest's and Walker's route is testimony to the extremes of technique and ethics attainable by today's climbers.

References

Ament, Pat. "The Black Canyon with Kor." *Mountain*, no. 50 (July/August 1976), pp. 20–23.

Chelton, Dudley, and Godfrey, Bob. *Climb!* Boulder, Colo.: Alpine House, 1977. Pp. 120, 133, and 135.

Forrest, Bill. "The Painted Wall." *Summit*, September 1973, pp. 14–19.

Forrest, Bill. Letter of December 1977.

Fricke, Walter W. "Black Canyon Yields Colorado's First Grade VI." *Off Belay*, no. 4 (August 1972), p. 45.

Karlstrom, Karl. "The Dragon Route." *Climbing*, July/August 1973, pp. 3–9.

Part 5

Giants

Just as there is a point at which rock climbing leaves off and mountaineering begins, so there is a point at which mountaineering leaves off and expeditioneering begins. High-altitude expeditioneering is a turning of the tables on the bulk of modern climbing. The dangers faced on most climbs are subjective—that is, they are within the control of the climber. A ticklish traverse, a series of A5 moves on skyhooks, a long runout on an overhanging face—these are artificial problems created by the climber. If he does not wish to face them, he can retreat.

In high-altitude expeditioneering, most of the dangers faced are objective dangers beyond the climber's control. These dangers include extreme cold, altitude-related illness, ice storms, high winds, whiteouts, avalanches, stonefall, hidden crevasses, and heavy snowfall. Unlike subjective dangers, objective dangers cannot be retreated from and left to another day. They can strike at any time, including the descent, and render the climber extremely vulnerable. Even well-organized expeditions, equipped with the best equipment and manned by experts, often lose members of their parties to the elements. In such climbing, stopping a fall is only a small part of the actions one must take in order to stay alive.

The diminutiveness of man is dramatically emphasized in expeditionary climbing. In an action that brings heroic myth and fable to mind, the climber dices with the principal forces of the planet, gambling that he can touch the nose of a giant and scurry back to safety with the fragile current of life still flowing within him. Expeditionary climbing is an answer to a call beyond the limits of human understanding. In adventures reminiscent of the earliest human epics, men seek their sirens on the fantasy crests of snowy peaks.

To answer this quasi-mystical call, explorers have sought the farthest regions of the globe. Patagonia, the Himalaya, the inner gray sections of sparsely settled continents, and the labyrinthine interiors of great ranges of unknown peaks all have their place in this puzzle. To most climbers, expeditionary climbing means a journey far beyond their native land.

American climbers are fortunate in having excellent expeditionary climbing in their own country, in the jet-age equivalent of their own backyard. The state of Alaska has among its abundance of environmental wealth great mountains unsurpassed by any others on earth. Although other mountains may be higher, more remote, or less climbed, the mountains of Alaska rise with a dramatic abruptness into frigid Arctic skies. *Majesty* is a word that describes their effect well.

It has been said that once a mountain has been climbed, it seems to let down its defenses. This is not so with the giants. Despite maps, radios, high-altitude rescue helicopters, and the best of training, one climbs the highest peaks on their terms only. To the highest peaks, a man will always be just a brief and insignficant spark. Here, perhaps, are the most permanent of frontiers.

19

Mount Saint Elias

On the feast day of Saint Elias, in 1741, Capt. Vitus Bering sighted a huge mountain from his ship, at anchor in the Gulf of Alaska. Christening the peak after the patron saint of the day, the captain made a note of it in his log, and the first of the Alaskan giants had been discovered.

As later explorers saw the peak, distinct in the clear, cold air, although 35 miles from the sea, its reputation grew. By the middle of the 19th century, it was rumored that Mount Saint Elias was the highest mountain in North America. In 1874 a government survey was made of the area, and the party reported Saint Elias' height as 19,600 feet. The effect of this report on alpinists was predictable. With a mountain thought to be the continent's highest so easy to approach by sea, the race was on to be first on top.

The first skirmish came in 1886, when the *New York Times*, eager to present a scientific image and gain some publicity at the same time, sponsored an expedition to the peak. This group sniffed about the seaward side of the mountain, advanced to a little more than 7,000 feet on its flanks, and turned back with the conviction that the summit would never be reached by man.

Two years later, a small international party got almost 4,000 feet higher before reaching the same conclusion and turning back.

To a geology professor named Israel Russell, however, these attempts only proved that the southwest side of the mountain was too formidable. He decided to attempt the north side, and in 1890, with the backing of the National Geographic Society and the U.S. Geological Survey, he set out for Alaska. Short on mountaineering experience and long on stamina, Russell and a partner, Mark Kerr, were beaten from the peak by a breakdown in logistics and a prolonged snowstorm.

Russell had not gained the peak, but he had gained a close look at the north side, and from this he planned a prospective route.

He returned in 1891 and followed a glacial basin to Russell Col, between Saint Elias and Mount Newton, but again his logistics were weak. The summit was definitely reachable, but if Russell and his party pressed on, they would be forced to descend in the dark. Doing so would sorely press their luck, and wisely but bitterly the group turned back.

The Russell excursions had not gained the summit, but they were not failures either. A route had been found which would take a party to the summit, and the primary exploratory purposes of the expeditions had been fulfilled. Among Russell's discoveries was a great mountain called Mount Logan. It was later determined to be 19,850 feet high, taller than Mount Saint Elias. At the time, however, top billing still went to Mount Saint Elias. The challenge was still there, and an answer was coming from Italy.

Prince Luigi Giuseppe Maria Fernando di Savoia-Aosta, duke of Abruzzi, was an adventurer's adventurer and a character fitting for the most fantastic novels of the day. He had traveled the world, commanded warships, and

Mount Saint Elias. (Courtesy Alaska Historical Library)

climbed the great peaks of Europe. He was dapper, kind, moderately modest, and extremely wealthy. In 1897, at the age of 24, he turned his attention to Mount Saint Elias.

Israel Russell had known the peak but did not know how to stage a large expedition. Abruzzi had mountaineering experience unexpected in one so young, and Russell's studies to serve him as a guide. With a 10-man party he came to Seattle and had Maj. E. S. Ingraham organize a 10-man team of porters. By yacht and commercial steamer, the group sailed for Alaska, where with more than 3,000 pounds of equipment they started up the Malaspina Glacier, using man-drawn sleds to pull their loads. Despite problems in sledding across heavily crevassed areas, the party made good time across the Malaspina, and then followed the Agassiz and Seward glaciers as well to the foot of the Newton Glacier, below Russell Col.

Almost two weeks of effort were necessary to move the duke's party up to Russell Col. Here, at 14,500 feet, he wisely camped and launched a well-planned summit push that put the entire party on top, despite widespread altitude sickness. After an investment of almost five months' time, the duke had climbed higher on the North American continent than any other man. He had not topped out the continent, however. In addition to the high mountain Professor Russell had seen from the Newton Glacier, prospectors in the Alaskan interior were returning with reports of a magnificently huge peak to the north. It was named Mount McKinley.

Regardless of altitude standings, Mount Saint Elias was no pushover. In fact, it was not climbed again for nearly half a century.

In 1946, an expedition from the Harvard Mountaineering Club was mounted on Mount Saint Elias. The team members were Dee and Kay Molenaar, who had climbed extensively in Washington; U.S. Army lieutenant Benjamin Ferris, the medical officer; Andrew and Betty Kauffman, who had climbed a great deal at Seneca Rocks and in the Washington, D.C., area; William Latady, who was in charge of supplies; and William Putnam, well known for his work with the American Alpine Club. The group was led by Maynard M. Miller.

The team planned a number of ambitious firsts, including the first American ascent of Mount Saint Elias, the first ascent of the mountain by the southwest ridge (scene of the unsuccessful 1886 and 1888 attempts), the first ascent of the mountain by females, and the first successful civilian use of military air support on an expedition.

The airdrops, courtesy of the U.S. Army Air Corps, proved quite helpful, decreasing the climbers' loads dramatically and providing some unexpected luxuries, such as fresh-baked apple pies from the bakery near the military air base. Through the airdrops, the expedition was able to save strength for the summit push and to gain extra mobility, as a result of which it was able to incorporate into its plans a first ascent of Mount Haydon, an 11,921-foot satellite of Mount Saint Elias.

Weather played a key role in the climb. On the Tyndall Glacier approach, the reflected sunlight from the snow raised temperatures into the 80s and sunburned any exposed flesh. On Mount Haydon, an ice field almost avalanched when the entire party was on it, resulting in a change of plans—climbing at night and camping during the unstable daytime. At the other extreme, a sudden and prolonged snowstorm trapped the climbers in their tents for a week, playing marathon poker games and praying for a break in the weather.

Later the initial summit bid was squelched when the peak became socked in and swirling snow heralded a new storm. Supply rationing began. Then the weather broke, and a new bid was made the following day.

This time, despite the climbers' severe altitude discomfort, the summit yielded. The joy of victory was tarnished by Bill Putnam's absence. Early in the summit bid, Putnam was compelled to abandon his valiant effort to climb at the high altitude despite a fairly recent war injury to his lungs. Yet all of the goals of the expedition were realized, as the rest of the team topped out on Mount Saint Elias on the 205th anniversary of its discovery by Vitus Bering. This resounding success was the result of careful planning and, given the setting, a large amount of luck.

With Alaskan statehood, Mount Saint Elias became a full-fledged American peak, although it holds dual citizenship. The southwest side, climbed by the Harvard group, is American soil, while the side climbed by the duke of Abruzzi now falls within a Canadian National Park. Mount Saint Elias remains a beautiful and challenging peak, and though its established height of 18,008 feet falls short of the height reported in 1874, the fact remains that the climber who can look out to the sea from its summit knows that he has achieved something of great worth.

References

Clark, Ronald W. *Men, Myths, and Mountains.* London: Weidenfeld and Nicolson, 1976. Pp. 132–35, 241, and 265.

Jones, Chris. *Climbing in North America.* Berkeley: University of California Press for American Alpine Club, 1976. Pp. 51–54.

Miles, John. "His Royal Highness." *Off Belay,* no. 33 (June 1977), pp. 6–11.

Miller, Maynard M. "First American Ascent of Mount Saint Elias." *National Geographic,* February 1948, pp. 229–48.

Anonymous. Note concerning first attempt on Mount Saint Elias, and subsequent discovery of Mount Logan. *North American Climber,* November 1975, p. 28.

Noyce, Wilfred, and McMorrin, Ian. *World Atlas of Mountaineering.* London: Thomas Nelson and Sons, 1969, Pp. 179–80.

Wood, Walter A. Letter to Editor. *Off Belay,* no. 35 (October 1977), p. 51.

20

Denali

In the 19th century as North America was explored, innumerable peaks and rises were thought by their discoverers to be the high point of the continent. The honor of the title was bestowed—sometimes simultaneously—on summits in the Wind River Range, the Colorado Rockies, the West Coast volcanoes, the Sierra Nevada, and the Canadian Rockies. Rumors of a gigantic mountain which dwarfed all contenders for the title were brought back by seafarers and prospectors who had been to Alaska, but these rumors were generally believed to be nothing more than the exaggerations of travelers. George Vancouver was one of the first to report the mountain's existence, in 1794, and Russian explorers were aware of it shortly thereafter. The Indians of Alaska had known of the mountain for many years and had placed it in their legends as the home of the sun. They called it Denali, "The Great One."

In the 1890s, a Princetonian named Dickey spotted the mountain while prospecting for gold. He named it for William McKinley, who had recently been nominated to

From the Alaska flatlands to the summit of Denali is the highest plains-to-peak rise of any mountain on earth. (Courtesy state of Alaska)

Denali and the Muldrow Glacier from the air. (Photo by Bill Truesdell, courtesy National Park Service)

run for the presidency. Soon after this sighting, hundreds of Alaskan prospectors were able to confirm tales of the mountain's existence, and the name Mount McKinley was designated official. Climbers have long preferred the Indian name, and public pressure will no doubt eventually result in the adoption of the far more enchanting Denali.

This time, there was little doubt that the highest mountain in North America had been found at last. The sheer scale of the peak was overwhelming, and although, measured from sea level, its summit is far lower than those of the Himalaya, its rise from the adjacent flatlands is a staggering 17,000 of its 20,320 feet, making Denali in this respect the highest mountain on earth.

Of course, climbers were soon in a race to reach the summit of this great peak. The first to try, in 1903, was James Wickersham, a judge from Fairbanks. Wicker-

Denali—the Great One—from Wonder Lake. (Photo by Jim Shives, courtesy National Park Service)

sham's party soon withdrew from contention, and that same year an attempt by Dr. Frederick Cook, the famed Arctic explorer, was also turned back by the mountain's Arctic defenses. Cook returned to the field in 1906, and spent several weeks with an exploration party on the south of the mountain, searching in vain for a route to the summit. Things were looking very doubtful indeed, but Cook set off with one porter for a last attempt on the summit. A few weeks later, Cook announced to the world that he had climbed the mountain in one eight-day push.

Belmore Brown and Herschel Parker, members of Cook's expedition, openly doubted his claim. In the following years, Cook was challenged on a number of fronts, and he answered all challenges with photographs of what he claimed was the summit of Denali. To settle the matter, Brown and Parker left the States for Alaska in 1909, where, miles from Denali, they were able to reproduce Cook's photographs on a relatively minor peak that was not even on the approach to the real top of the continent. Having thus proved Cook to be a liar, they tried to climb Denali themselves, failed, and returned to hear news of yet another claim. Tom Lloyd, a Fairbanks native, maintained that he and three other Alaska sourdoughs had climbed the North Peak of Denali and had left the Stars and Stripes on a 14-foot flagpole at the summit as evidence of their conquest.

This seemed to be another farce. Lloyd reported that he and his companions—none of whom were available to confirm his story—had lived in the field by hunting and fishing, made the ascent with homemade mountaineering equipment, and done the final 9,000 feet in one 18-hour push, from camp to peak and back. These claims, together with the idea of making the climb with a flagpole 14 feet long and 4 inches thick at its base, invited even less acceptance than had Cook's fabrication.

Brown and Parker were back again in 1912, to make another attempt on Denali and to investigate the latest summit claim. The weather was not with them, however, and they called a retreat below the summit.

The next year, a party composed of Archdeacon Hudson Stuck, Harry Karsten, Walter Harper, and Robert Tatum came to Denali. Following what is now called Karsten's Ridge, the four proceeded with difficulty, as the ridge had been shattered by an earthquake just after Parker's and Brown's retreat in 1912. Weeks later, on June 6, they made the final push to the summit of the South Peak of Denali. The mountain had at last been climbed, but even more amazing, the summit party clearly saw the tattered shreds of what had once been an American flag, flying from a 14-foot flagpole on the slightly lower North Peak.

Since the first ascent of Denali, the mountain has been the target of hundreds of expeditions. It has been used for the purpose of scientific observation, and it has served as a testing ground for military cold-weather gear. It has been climbed by mountaineers from every major nation with a mountaineering tradition and by teams of women, the first expedition of this type, in 1970, being that of the "Denali Damsels"—Arlene Blum, Margaret Young, Dana Isherwood, Faye Kerr, and Margaret Clark. Denali has been climbed by large expeditions, and it has been soloed. In 1976, Tayomi Oishi skied all the way from the summit to the airstrip sector of the Kahiltna Glacier. That same year, three climbers made what may well remain the ultimate descent, using specially designed hang gliders to sail from the summit to the glacier.

The numerous stunts, firsts, and fiascos that take place on Denali each year are misleading in light of the actual character of the mountain. For some, the ascent of Denali has been pleasant and straightforward. For others, it has been a classic alpine struggle, with days of storm and hardship before the summit was gained. For many, the summit has been unattainable. And for far too many, Denali has been a nightmare, dealing out pain and even death.

Much of the tragedy that Denali has meted out over the years has been a result of pure stupidity. Denali is a high mountain in a hostile climate, and those who climb it face the combined hazards of alpine dangers and Arctic wilder-

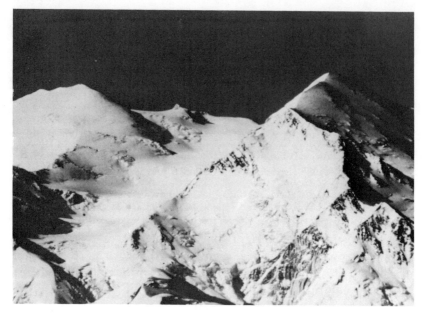

The twin summits of Denali, with the true summit to the left. (Courtesy National Park Service)

ness. Denali's northern location makes its upper portions as cold and hostile as the upper portions of mountains in southern regions which are several thousands of feet higher. Avalanches, crevasses, unimaginable cold, high winds, prolonged storms, deep snow, dehydration, a host of high-altitude illnesses, and severe disorientation are just a sampling of the misfortunes that a climber may encounter on Denali. Moreover, when disaster does strike, it is often impossible for help to arrive in time to be of any assistance. Rescue parties often require several days to reach an accident site; only rarely can helicopters be of any use, since the air near the top of Denali is beyond their ceiling altitude; and the mountain is often too storm-swept for air travel. Climbers who have ascended lesser peaks on the strength of pure luck often discover that on Denali their luck has run out. A lack of preparation means trouble.

The first step toward a successful and safe Denali expedition is foreknowledge of the conditions that one will encounter. Mountaineering journals give up-to-date reports on new routes on Denali (and other mountains), as well as detailed accounts from expeditions which have climbed the mountain. The accounts of many Denali expeditions are available in book form, and the various expedition accounts, photographic surveys, maps, histories, and guides published by one author, Bradford Washburn, constitute what is probably the best and most complete body of information concerning Denali that is available anywhere. Mount McKinley National Park, within which the bulk of Denali is located, keeps information and expedition accounts from every Denali expedition, and climbers are welcome to use this expedition file in planning their climbs. The park officials are also quite willing to answer any questions that prospective climbers may have after these climbers have reviewed the available literature, and will generally refer climbers with questions that they cannot answer to experienced Denali climbers who can. Persons who plan to climb Mount McKinley National Park peaks should communicate frankly and openly to the park administration any questions that they may have about the climb they are planning. The members of the park staff have a stake in every expedition planned, as sooner or later it is they who must clean up the aftermaths of disaster.

Once they have compiled the necessary information, would-be Denali climbers should organize their expedition team carefully. The team should consist of climbers who are experienced in winter alpine climbing and high-altitude work, especially for the more difficult routes. It is also important that the team members know and get along well with one another, since the members of expeditions organized by mail must often do battle with one another as well as with the mountain. Once a team has been formed, a leader chosen by the team must submit a request to climb the route selected, no later than 60 days before the

Camp on Denali at 17,000 feet.
(Courtesy National Park Service)

climb, along with physicians' statements and detailed mountaineering histories for each member of the team. This information must be on special forms that the park will provide and explain on request. Each expedition must also have a name, and only one person may act as spokesman for the team, to avoid confusion or the duplication of paperwork. Obviously, 60 days is a bare minimum of time for the processing of all this information, and it is smart for teams to begin the registration process a year or so before the actual climb.

Equipment preparation should be taken care of next, with radio equipment a priority, since the arrangements for radio communications equipment (and such equipment is mandatory for all expeditions) take a long time to complete. Attention should then be given to cold-weather clothing, particularly boots. More than 10 percent of the people who climbed Denali during a test season suffered frostbite severe enough to require hospitalization. The best

The summit of Denali seen from 17,600 feet. (Courtesy National Park Service)

footwear for the prevention of frostbite is the military Korean boot. Next in order of effectiveness are expedition double boots and civilian Korean boots. Persons who wear standard mountaineering boots on Denali can expect to lose toes, and possibly their limbs or their lives. This is a cold mountain. Down parkas, pants, and mittens of expedition weight and length are essential, and down booties are good for campwear. Hats, face masks, and silk under-gloves are recommended by the National Park Service for protection against wind, sun, and cold. Parkas should have hoods; woolen clothing should be worn under the down; and wind pants are necessary, as are extra mittens. For warmth in all conditions woolen underclothing and socks should be worn, and expedition-quality sleeping bags with good foam or hide pads are the only ways to ensure proper rest in the cold Alaskan night. An extra pair of snow-and-sun goggles should be carried in case of loss, and surprisingly enough, mosquito nets and raingear will be needed

Climbers above 11,000 feet.
(Courtesy National Park Serivce)

for parties coming from Wonder Lake to the north—Mount McKinley National Park is not all mountain.

For shelter, expedition-style tents should be carried, and tents that are a little bit larger than necessary (that is, a four-man tent for every two persons) will be more comfortable during long storms. The group should have at least two snow shovels (grain scoops) and two snow saws, since these are keys to survival when storms require the excavation of camps or snow caves or the construction of igloos. It is important that expedition members learn how to build snow shelters before going onto the mountain. Snowshoes are used for travel, though for skiers who are experienced at ski-mountaineering, metal-edged mountaineering skis are as good as, if not better than, snowshoes. Extra snowshoes or skis are a good idea, and spare ice axes and crampons, the other two travel essentials, should also be carried.

Kerosene seems to be the best bet for cooking at high altitudes, though white gas is sometimes a good alterna-

An expedition camp on Denali. (Courtesy National Park Service)

tive. Gas-cartridge stoves do not work in extreme cold, and a spare stove is a good way to keep hot meals and melted water available, with two stoves per party a minimum acceptable number. Waterproof matches and butane lighters (carried in an inside pocket so that they'll work) will be needed to light stoves. Cook kits should be big enough to cook meals and melt water, and candle lanterns are the best source of light to cook and eat by, since flashlights soon fail in the cold.

The expedition's food supply should be palatable at high altitudes, suitable for extraquick cooking, plentiful, prepackaged in easily handled containers, and higher in calories than is the food eaten at sea level. The meal lists of successful expeditions should be consulted, and it should be remembered that weather problems can significantly lengthen the time spent in the field, thus increasing the number of meals needed. Heat-sealed heavy plastic bags are the best general food containers, and packaging entire individual meals avoids rooting around at mealtime and prevents food loss and spoilage.

The climbing gear needed will vary according to the route planned, but all routes will require at least 350 wands for trail-marking, one standard-length nine millimeter rope for every two persons, low-stretch rope sufficient for any area requiring fixed lines (with some extra for replacing lost or buried fixed ropes), and a good selection of snow pickets and ice screws, with a carabiner for each picket or screw and at least three extra carabiners per person.

For emergency use and field maintenance, each person should have a standard personal first-aid kit, as well as any needed medication (with spare prescriptions carried by the group leader), glacier cream, sunscreen, painkillers, and antibiotics. A larger group medicine kit should be

Mount Foraker and the Kahiltna Glacier from 17,000 feet. (Courtesy National Park Service)

assembled with the help of a physician, and it is wise to include sleeping pills in this kit, since the altitude may keep some of the climbers awake. Repair kits should be assembled for use in emergencies involving equipment, and a signal kit that includes smoke bombs, flares, mirrors, and colored panels should be made up for general use.

When assembling equipment, it is wise to think out each item in terms of what is needed with what and to plan multiple use as much as possible. For example stoves require fuel, fuel containers, such spare parts as extra valve keys, stove carrying containers, insulation to prevent heat loss, starting paste, and matches. However, some cook kits are made so that stoves can fit inside them, eliminating the need for extra containers, and a closed-cell foam sleeping pad will work as stove insulation, eliminating the need for an extra stove pad.

Looking down Karsten's Ridge. (Courtesy National Park Service)

A final step in equipment preparation is to try everything out in the field and then to inspect all items carefully before packaging them for shipment to Mount McKinley National Park. This may seem obvious, but many forget to do it. If there is any doubt about equipment, a park climbing ranger will be glad to check a group's gear before the climb.

Obviously, for all but lightweight alpine expeditions a Denali climb requires more gear than the climbers can carry at one time. On the mountain this is taken care of by ferrying loads from camp to camp, but ferrying loads to the mountain is too time consuming, and outside help will be needed.

Parties starting climbs on the north or west side of Denali will probably get equipment to the mountain by hiring a horse packer to carry the gear from Wonder Lake, past the McKinley River, to a cache site near the first camp. Those climbing routes on the south or east side will probably transport both gear and team by aircraft to the "Kahiltna International," an area of the Kahiltna Glacier which is outside the park and is used as an airstrip by expeditions. With possible exceptions for purely scientific expeditions, no air support of any kind is allowed within the national park.

Expedition leaders must check in in person or by phone with park headquarters just before and just after the climb. Climbers should avoid jetting to Fairbanks, calling in, and then flying to the Kahiltna in a space of one or two days. Resting up before flying in will put a more alert team on the glacier, and spending a day at the staging area will make the altitude a little easier to take.

On the mountain, time must be budgeted carefully and the team must be a team in every sense of the term. Simple things, such as cooking meals, will take longer, even with the chores divided up efficiently. The high altitudes will slow mental processes significantly, necessitating discussion even for simple decisions, and motivation will decrease as height is gained, so team encouragement and work distribution will be needed in order to keep the climb from falling apart. A team mentality is also a safeguard, as the expedition is its own primary rescue source. Nothing outside the group can be absolutely relied on to provide help on Denali.

If a team of climbers are prepared to deal sensibly with high-altitude Arctic alpine conditions, and if they are ready and able to rescue themselves from avalanches, crevasses, falls, storms, and medical emergencies, they stand a very good chance of getting off Denali in good health. If they are capable, and if the weather is with them, they will probably make the summit with few problems.

This may sound too pessimistic, but the records of several Denali expeditions show that a lack of teamwork and preparation can be a bad thing on this Alaskan giant.

At 12,000 feet, looking toward Peters Glacier. (Courtesy National Park Service)

Backpack, ice ax, snowshoes, and a sled—glacier travel on Denali. (Courtesy National Park Service)

A good example of this is the Joseph F. Wilcox Expedition, which attempted Denali in 1967. This group had 12 members and it should have been very strong, but inexperience among its members and a lack of team preparation made it weak. Of the group's 12 members, only 5 lived to make it off Denali.

The best routes for expeditions making first trips to Denali are the *Muldrow Route*, from the north, and the *West Buttress*, from the south. These are the least technically demanding routes on the mountain, and a popular traverse has been to pack in from Wonder Lake, climb the *Muldrow* to the summit, and descend via the *West Buttress* to the Kahiltna International for the fly-out. This is a good way to see several aspects of Denali in a combination of adventures.

Guided expeditions on Denali are often offered by qualified organizations, and these are often advertised in the mountaineering journals. Guided groups have higher success rates than do private ventures, and they enable the climber who cannot raise a qualified group to climb the mountain in relative safety.

Mount McKinley Climber's Guide, published by the Alaska Alpine Company in Anchorage, is a good place to start gathering information for a climb.

Denali is one of the largest and most beautiful mountains in the world. With proper preparation, it can also be one of the most memorable climbs in a climbing career, with neither the mountain nor the climber the loser.

References

Baldwin, Ralph. "The Crisis on Denali." *Off Belay*, no. 30 (December 1976), pp. 2–10.

Becker, Terry; Bocarde, Gary; and Hale, Jim. "An Open Letter to Prospective Mount McKinley Climbers." *Mountain*, no. 55 (May/June 1977), p. 46.

Bertulis, Alex. "Mount McKinley's South Face, Alpine Style." *Mountain*, no. 28 (July 1973), pp. 24–29.

Blum, Arlene. "The Damsels and Denali." *Summit*, May 1971, pp. 18–26.

Clark, Ronald W. *Men, Myths, and Mountains*. London: Weidenfeld and Nicolson, 1976. Pp. 134–38.

Hackett, Steve W. "Mount McKinley Summary." *Off Belay*, no. 10 (August 1973), p. 43.

Jones, Chris. *Climbing in North America*. Berkeley: University of California Press for American Alpine Club, 1976. Pp. 55–67, 255–65.

McMorrin, Ian, and Noyce, Wilfred. *World Atlas of Mountaineering*. London: Thomas Nelson and Sons, 1969. P. 180.

Matthews, William H., III. *A Guide to the National Parks*. Garden City, N.Y.: Natural History Press, 1968. Vol. 1, pp. 225–38.

Anonymous. "More on National Parks." *Off Belay*, no. 21 (June 1975), pp. 39–41.

Mount McKinley National Park. "Mountaineering Mount McKinley National Park, Alaska" (information booklet).

Schenck, Jeb. "Mount McKinley—Littered and Overcrowded Route." *Summit*, December 1970, pp. 24–25.

Scott, Doug. "Adventure on McKinley." *Mountain*, no. 52 (November/December 1976), pp. 19–21.

Snyder, Howard H. *The Hall of the Mountain King*. New York: Charles Scribner's Sons, 1973.

Williams, Kendall. "McKinley Odyssey." *Climbing*, March/April 1974, pp. 16–20.

Appendix A
Rating Systems

Throughout this book, I have indicated the ratings of various climbs through the use of the Yosemite Decimal System, a numerical system based upon the older Sierra Club System for rating the relative difficulty of a technical climb. Like most such rating systems the Yosemite Decimal System does not rate the difficulty of an entire climb, but simply measures the difficulty of the hardest move, or crux, of the climb, on the theory that a climber who can do the crux can do the climb. Practice does not always follow theory, however, and extended climbs are generally more difficult than briefer climbs, regardless of the crux rating. For this reason, the Yosemite Decimal System has been amended by the Grade System, to indicate roughly the amount of time involved in doing a climb.

The Grade System is pretty easy to understand—the higher the number, the longer the climb. The breakdown is as follows:

I.   The climb will take two hours or less, and it involves about two leads, or less than 300 feet of climbing.

II. The climb will take from two to four hours, and it can go up to five leads, or 500 feet of climbing.
III. The climb will take most of a day, and can involve usually more than five leads, or several hundred feet of climbing.
IV. The climb will take all day, and it may take a little more than a day. The climbers should be prepared to bivouac.
V.   The climb will definitely take more than a day for the average party. Fixed ropes or bivouac gear and supplies will be needed.
VI. This is a big wall climb or an extended mountaineering route that will take a number of days and the climbers should be prepared accordingly.

All of these grades assume a party of from two to four or more persons, as well as climbing in the mid-to-upper ranges of difficulty, being done by climbers of average to upper-average abilities.

The Yosemite Decimal System is a bit harder to understand, since it is an extension of an earlier system which rated climbs from class 1 to class 6 and simply put all technical climbing in class 5 and all aid climbing in class 6. The YDS divides class 5 climbing into subclasses by adding a suffix to the rating. Originally, this was done by running the system from 5.0 to 5.9, with 5.0 being easy and 5.9 being quite hard. Soon, however, climbs above the 5.9 rating were being done. The system could not go to 6, as this would indicate aid, so the somewhat illogical rating of 5.10 was added, not to be confused with 5.1. As this rating was passed, 5.11 and 5.12 were added, and the once-closed system began to show signs of being open-ended. Basically, one need only remember that the 5 before the decimal point means that a climb is technical and that the number after the decimal point means that the climb is easy or hard, with higher numbers meaning harder climbs. Thus 5.0 would indicate a good route for teaching one's grandmother to climb on, whereas 5.12 is fast approaching the realm of suction cups and antigravity machines. A few years ago an attempt was made to amend the YDS with further letter suffixes to indicate protection quality; this system never caught on, and it will not be dealt with here.

To confuse those who are not already baffled, I am also furnishing a comparison of the Yosemite Decimal, the British, and the Australian rating systems. The UIAA (Union Internationale des Associations Alpines) system will not be gone into here, since most people using it are also familiar with the British system. Also excluded is the National Climbing Congress System, which went out with soft pitons and steel carabiners in all but a few eccentric areas of the country. Persons who wish to see comparisons of the UIAA and NCCS systems can find them in most guidebooks. The British system is shown here because it is descriptive, and the Australian system is included because it is straightforward and open-ended and because someday it may be adopted as a standard international rating system:

YDS	Australian	British	Comments
1	1	Easy	Trail-walking
2	2	Easy	Rough trail (scree)
3	3	Moderate	Hands used
4	4	Moderate	Rope used without running belays
5.0	5	Difficult	Running belays used; fall can be fatal
5.1	6	Difficult	
5.2	7	Very difficult	
5.3	8	Very difficult	
5.4	9	Very difficult	
5.4	10	Very difficult	
5.5	11	Very difficult	Average difficulty
5.5	12	Severe	

YDS	Australian	British	Comments
5.6	13	Very severe	
5.6	14	Very severe	
5.7	15	Very severe	
5.7	16	Hard very severe	
5.8	17	Hard very severe	Upper difficulty
5.8	18	Hard very severe	
5.9	19	Hard very severe	
5.9	20	Extremely severe	
5.10	21	Extremely severe	Extreme climbing
5.10	22	Extremely severe	
5.10	23	Extremely severe	
5.11	24	Extremely severe	
5.11	25	Extremely severe	
5.11	26	Extremely severe	
5.12	27	Extremely severe	
5.12	28	Extremely severe	
5.13	29	Extremely severe	

It should be noted that these systems actually have no direct correlation and that in the upper levels especially, there will be differences of opinion as to what ratings in the systems are equivalent.

In the YDS, a plus sign (+) is often used to indicate a climb that is hard for the rating, and I have used this notation several times in this book. It is also customary to assume that a climb with no grade notation is Grade III or lower. There are exceptions, of course. When discussing big-wall climbs, it is assumed that one is talking about a high-grade route, whether or not grade is mentioned.

That takes care of free climbing. Now we come to aid climbing. Aid is indicated by the capital letter A after the free climbing designation. The number following the letter indicates the security of the placement being climbed on, with the exception of A0, which indicates a grabbed piton or something of the sort. The rule is: the higher the number, the less secure the placement. Thus, A1 is a placement that would serve well as a protection placement; A2 could hold a fall if it were required to; A3 holds body weight but would not stop a fall; A4 will hold body weight if the gods are not displeased; and A5 is a succession of A4 placements.

Thus, a climb that involves mid-range free climbing with a fair-to-marginal aid section and takes a day or more to complete would be listed as IV, 5.5, A3.

Finally, I should warn the reader not to take route ratings as Gospel. Ratings may vary slightly from area to area, and ratings take no note of whether a climber is short, tall, stout, or large-footed. Also, ratings make no distinction between a 5.10 strength move and a 5.10 balance move. I have had the unreliability of ratings demonstrated to me on many occasions, on one of which I lost the route on a 5.4 and took a zipping head-over-heels leader fall, then climbed what was supposedly a respectable 5.7 without being able to find a crux. In the end, climbs boil down to "Fine for me," "Too easy," and "Way too hard," and rating systems should always be regarded simply as general indicators.

Appendix B
Glossary

Abseil: To rope down after a climb; often used to describe a free rappel.

Aid: Climbing on equipment rather than directly on rock; also, to employ such technique or to employ an equipment placement for such climbing.

Alpenstock: A metal-shod staff carried by most 19th century climbers.

Arete: A sharply sloped and narrow ridge.

Avalanche cord: A brightly colored small-diameter rope. In case of avalanche, the end not attached to the mountaineer is thrown downslope, in the hope that rescuers will follow the cord to the victim.

Bat Hook: A sky hook driven into a drilled hole.

Belay: To protect from a possible fall; also, the technique used in such protection.

Bivouac: To spend a night on a climb with minimal or marginal shelter, often done by sleeping in hammocks; also, the name for such a stay.

Bivouac sack: A waterproof survival shelter for bivouacs in inclement weather; also called "bivvy sack."

Bolt: A metal device for protection or aid that is ham-

199

mered or screwed into a hole drilled in the rock; also, to place such a device.

Bolt ladder: A series of bolt placements employed to pass blank sections of rock.

Bombproof: Solid or very secure; used to describe good holds, protection placements, investments, etc.

Bouldering: A demanding, gymnastic type of climbing done on small faces and boulders, in which the objectives are skill and grace, rather than simply reaching the top.

Cairn: A pile of rocks built on a summit to commemorate a successful ascent.

Carabiner: A metal device similar to a chain link in appearance, with a gate in one side to admit slings, other carabiners, rope, etc.; used like a portable metal knot to join pieces of a protection system.

Chimney: A three-sided vertical fault in a face, large enough to admit a climber's body.

Chock: A clean-climbing protection device wedged into cracks; short for "artificial chockstone."

Chockstone: A stone which is placed or has fallen into a crack; often tied off with a sling for protection.

Clean climbing: Climbing done without scarring or marring the rock or the habitat surrounding the rock.

Couloir: A deep mountain gorge.

Crampon: A spiked device placed on the boot for purchase on ice or hard snow.

Crux: The hardest part of a pitch or climb.

Dike: A crack or cavity in the rock which has been filled with igneous materials.

Dog routes: The usual routes for novices in a given place; also called "tourist routes."

Dynamic: Descriptive of a type of climbing that is dependent upon motion for added force and reach, such as climbing involving hand-to-hand swings.

EBs: A popular brand of friction shoe; other popular brands include PAs, RRs, and RDs.

Escarpment: A steep slope or cliff line, often at the edge of a plateau.

Etriers: Ladderlike stirrup devices, formed from slings and used as handholds and footholds in aid work.

Exposure: Climber's euphemism for the air beneath one's heels on a climb or the apparent amount of air beneath one's heels; climbs with a great deal of such space are called "exposed."

Face: The largest definable subsection of a mountain or a rock formation.

Face climbing: To climb a rock face.

Flake: A detached or semidetached piece of rock lying close to the main rock mass.

Free: To climb without aid; often used as an adjective for such climbing.

Free solo: To climb without aid or protection; sometimes called "third-classing" in reference to class 3 climbing in the Yosemite Decimal System, though free soloing is generally nonprotected climbing of a fifth-class route.

Friction shoes: Tightly fitting shoes with soft rubber bottoms, which give extra purchase and dexterity on smooth rock.

Gendarme: A rock pillar which hinders ridge travel; also used to describe ice formations presenting similar problems.

Grade: Properly, the time or distance length of a climb, though the term is commonly used synonymously with *rate*.

Hypothermia: A sudden and often fatal drop in the core temperature of the body due to exposure.

Igneous: Geologic term for material formed from molten rock.

Jam: A hold where the hand or foot is caught corklike in a crack.

Lead: To go first on the rope or to climb in such a fashion that one person is without a rope from above; also, the distance climbed during one person's turn at such climbing.

Mantle: Short for mantleshelf, a technique in which the climber mounts a ledge like a swimmer leaving a pool.

Massif: An identifiably whole group of mountains, with one peak as an apex.

Nailing: Driving pitons.

Nuts: Artificial chockstones, so called because the first artificial chockstones were common machine nuts.

Peneplain: Land leveled by erosion.

Pendulum: To swing across a face on a rope, usually done to reach a parallel crack system from another crack which has played out.

Pin: Euphemism for a piton.

Pitch: The distance traveled in one lead, usually almost a rope-length.

Piton: A metal instrument designed to be driven by hammer into an existing crack in rock, for use as an anchor.

Protection: The system, and the parts thereof, used by climbers to safeguard against the consequences of a fall.

Rappel: A controlled descent down a rope, employing body- or device-generated friction as a braking aid; when done improperly, referred to as "falling."

Rating: An estimation of a particular climb's degree of difficulty, on the basis of the most difficult move required in the climb.

Roof: A piece of rock jutting far out from a cliff, over-hanging the cliff section below it; a very large overhang.

Runout: The distance traveled on a climb since the last protection placement.

Saddle: A bowed ridge between two summits.

Schist: A metamorphic rock consisting of flakelike layers.

Sedimentary: Rock formed by the deposit of settling materials such as sandstone.

Skyhook: An aid device attached to stirrups and hooked onto small irregularities in the rock.

Squeeze chimney: To ascend a narrow chimney by wriggling upward serpentlike; also, a chimney requiring such technique.

Static: Descriptive of nondynamic climbing, in which holds are purchased without swings or thrusts.

Stem: To climb with one limb extended almost sideways to an opposite wall or hold, as a balance point.

Supergaiter: A gaiter covering the boot from the sole up, used for extra warmth in winter climbing.

Technical climbing: Climbing requiring the use of rope and specialized knowledge and equipment.

Testpiece: a route indicative of an area standard.

Third class: Ropeless climbing; euphemism for free soloing.

Top-rope: To climb belayed from above.

Wand: A rod or dowel, usually topped by a small flag or a bright splash of color, used to mark routes in snow climbing.

Whiteout: A condition of dense fog, cloud, or snow, in which it is impossible to gauge one's surroundings by sight.

Index